First published in Great Britain in 2002 by
YOUNG WRITERS
Remus House,
Coltsfoot Drive,
Peterborough, PE2 9JX
Telephone (01733) 890066

HB ISBN 0 75433 852 5
SB ISBN 0 75433 853 3

FOREWORD

This year, the Young Writers' Hidden Treasures competition proudly presents a showcase of the best poetic talent from over 72,000 up-and-coming writers nationwide.

Young Writers was established in 1991 and we are still successful, even in today's technologically-led world, in promoting and encouraging the reading and writing of poetry.

The thought, effort, imagination and hard work put into each poem impressed us all, and once again, the task of selecting poems was a difficult one, but nevertheless, an enjoyable experience.

We hope you are as pleased as we are with the final selection and that you and your family continue to be entertained with *Hidden Treasures West Sussex Vol I* for many years to come.

Contents

The Poems

CROCKY'S MEAL

Crocky the crocodile loves to eat,
He loves horse stew on the highest heat.
He could eat a delicious lamb,
And have room left for a slice of ham.
He adores his scrumptious pork,
But he doesn't use a knife and fork.
One sunny day when he left the lake,
In search of something huge to bake,
He suddenly saw his gigantic meal,
On a big rock in a fresh, green field.
It was a lion with a beautiful mane,
And Lawrence was the lion's name.
'Hello old lion!' Crocky said,
'I'm really desperate to be fed,
Why don't you come along with me?
I'll show you where to eat, you'll see!'
'I can't,' said the lion to old Crock,
'For I am stuck to this 'ere rock,
But if you come and help me free,
I'm sure I'll help you find some tea.'
So over came Crocky the croc,
To free the lion from his rock.
But just as Crocky got his prey,
The lion suddenly started to say,
'I've got you Crocky, you can't come free,
You're coming down my throat, you'll see!'
Crunch, crunch, crunch went the lion's jaws,
As he scratched Crocky with his claws.
Soon Lawrence the lion stopped his munch,
For he had finished all his lunch!

Helen Turner (11)
Arunside County Primary School

Pets All Over The Place

Chickens in the garden
Scratching in the mud
Sometimes accidentally digging up a spud.

Rabbits on the patio
Hopping round the run
Fluffy baby bunnies are a great deal of fun.

Mice in the bedroom
Phew, what a pong!
Thankfully the cleaning doesn't take long.

Gerbils in the living room
Shredding up paper
Let them out to run to have a little caper.

Fish in the pond
Coming up to feed
Mind they don't get tangled in the waterweed.

Serena Dalton (11)
Arunside County Primary School

Teachers

School is a fun place to be,
All the teachers are the best,
Teachers, teachers never rest,
My teacher is a funny man,
I don't expect he has many fans,
I know he has one, that's me,
But teachers, teachers are the *best.*

Emma Hearn (9)
Birdham CE Primary School

My Dog!

I have a dog called Arnie
I think he's rather barmy
He loves to run and has lots of fun
He's fit enough to be in the army.

He's got big brown eyes and a squashed up face
His lips hang down but don't look out of place
When I am sad
He comes over to me and makes me glad.

He hates wearing hats and loves chasing cats
When he wants a walk
I think he tries to talk
I love my dog Arnie!

Lauren Gowing (9)
Birdham CE Primary School

Mr Kartoffel

Mr Kartoffel's a whimsical man,
He sits in the cooker to get a good tan.
He fries his snot,
Then eats the lot.
When it comes to the night,
He sleeps on the bright light.
Then he burns his bum,
And looks very glum.
So he sits in the freezer,
And turns into a geezer.

Maria Edwards (10)
Birdham CE Primary School

My Guinea Pig

I have a little guinea pig
He's really rather sweet
He's black and brown
He has a twitching nose
And tiny little feet!

He lives in a hutch
And he eats so much
He eats apples, carrots
And guinea pig food
He eats so much it's hardly chewed!

So that he can play
I put him in his run
And then he goes back in his hutch
When the day is done!

Madalaine Gowing (9)
Birdham CE Primary School

Mr Kartoffel

Mr Kartoffel's a whimsical man
He fries his waste in a frying pan
He eats off of slate
Instead of a plate
He cleans his teeth with an ink eraser
Thank goodness for us his name is not Frazier
At night he sleeps in his neighbour's bed
He uses the grill to melt his big head
To put it in the right shape
He starts to scrape.

Amy Morgan (10)
Birdham CE Primary School

THE SEASONS

Thank you God for the silver snow,
For the glittering, silver frost,
For the tweeting robin
And the beautiful holly leaves with the lovely, red berries.

Thank you God for the fresh, new grass,
For the leaping lambs and the chirping larks,
For the daffodil trumpets, trumpeting loud,
And little new chicks jumping proud.

Thank you God for the hot, bright sun,
For my trips to the seaside that are fun, fun, fun!
For the beautiful flowers that grow in the garden,
For the bumblebees busy buzzing loudly.

Thank you God for the crunchy, crisp leaves,
For the animals collecting nuts and berries,
For the whole country getting ready for winter in warm clothes,
For the night coming quickly and twinkling stars.

Thank you God for the seasons.

Bethany Andrews (8)
Birdham CE Primary School

THEY CAME

In they came with pride
As the gallant knight approached
Darkness fell on war.

Ben Wright (9)
Birdham CE Primary School

Christmas Poem

Christmas is a happy time,
When people try to look fine.
I like Christmas because it's fun,
I always jump about and run.
We open our presents under the tree,
And everyone shouts, 'What's for me?'
We're all so excited,
And we just can't hide it!

Lucy Ford (8)
Birdham CE Primary School

The Tale Of The Hidden Treasure

My friend the fisherman
As old as the Earth
Told me a story
Worth listening to.

He told me of treasure
Shimmering like gold
Bound in a chest
Ready for me to find.

My friend tells me of
The treasure inside
Rubies, diamonds, emeralds and pearls
I would love to find it.

Charlie Clark (9)
Bishop Tufnell Junior School

THE TREASURE UNDER THE SEA

I'm as hot as a volcano and feeling so dim
So I have decided to go for a swim.

I am diving in by one of my mighty cannonballs
And the water is as cold as a little ice cube sat in a big, cold freezer.

I'm now diving to the bottom of the deep blue sea
Oh, what's that!

Oh wow! It's a lovely, violet, little shell
So I open it up to find a lovely, shiny, creamy, silvery pearl
As smooth as silk.

I'm getting rather cold now so I better go.

I wonder if that was the treasure Nanny was talking about?
I wonder, I wonder, I wonder?

Lee Rainey (9)
Bishop Tufnell Junior School

WATER POEM

Sharks swimming elegantly
Oysters showing off their pearls
Sea urchins gliding through the water
Blue whales smelling like a thousand years old
Fish looking like a rainbow
Coral beds looking like multicoloured cream
Seaweed smelling like a thousand-year-old sock
A storm is brewing.

Ben Odin (8)
Bishop Tufnell Junior School

Under Sea Treasure

I opened my door
Hey, where is my floor?
Cool, look it's water
It's full of fish, dolphins and electric eels
I wonder if it's my imagination
I rub my eyes
And to my surprise
The water is still there.

I dive in with my clothes on
And swim along
I go further and further until my door is out of sight
Oh look, it's oysters!
They're opening and inside there are dazzling pearls
They're as clear as crystal.

I have to have one
I swim closer and closer and I've got one
I swim around to see if I can find anything else
What's that I see? Could it be . . .
Yes it is, it's diamonds, rubies, emeralds, gold, silver and pearls
Wow!

Rachel Baggs (9)
Bishop Tufnell Junior School

My Treasure - My Cat

My treasure is soft, furry and grey
With pointy and sharp claws
Her eyes are caramel colour
Soft pink pads on her paws.

At dawn her bell jingles
As she walks along the floor
It's six o'clock in the morning
She's miaowing at the door.

Sam Taylor (8)
Bishop Tufnell Junior School

Treasure From The Sea

I'm going to Atlantis
To find the hidden gold
The city is so ancient
It's older than old.

When I got there
It was so bright
It really did
Give me a fright.

I think it was bright
Because I had found the treasure
I had to reach the surface though
Too great was the pressure.

I took it to the jeweller
To see if it was rare
And luckily for me
He said that it was scarce.

I took it home
To keep it a mystery
So even if you search
It is now history.

Joshua Bappoo (8)
Bishop Tufnell Junior School

Treasure In The Sea

I'm looking for a pretty pearl
At the bottom of the sea
It's as precious as a diamond
I'm sure it's meant for me.

It just has to be somewhere
Maybe somewhere in the sand
I'm rummaging, rummaging all over the ocean floor
I wish I could feel it in my hand.

I saw an oyster
Then I saw something glinting inside
I found the treasure, I found it
Now it can't hide.

I'm going to the surface
I know what I'm going to do with it
Yes I know, I know
I'll pass it down to my children!

Matthew Cole (9)
Bishop Tufnell Junior School

Hidden Gem

While digging in my garden
I saw something sparkling blue
In the cold, damp earth
It was covered in brown mud
I picked it up
Was it thousands of years old?

Thomas Gamester (9)
Bishop Tufnell Junior School

Under The Ocean

I swam through the ocean
Searching everywhere
Looking for the place where
The precious pearls were hidden.

There a whale was guarding
The pearls as smooth as silk
But the whale-like huge mountains
Wouldn't let me get the precious pearls.

I didn't give up though
I couldn't get through
The coral as hard as rock
Wouldn't let me have the precious pearls.

But a hole through the back
Was just the right size
To squeeze through, hooray!
I had the precious pearls.

Charlotte Wainwright (9)
Bishop Tufnell Junior School

Hidden Treasure

Hidden, hidden, hidden it is
It is probably older than old
And it sparkles in the moonlight.

Hidden, hidden, hidden it is
It is as bright as gold
And now I have got the hidden treasure.

Toby James (9)
Bishop Tufnell Junior School

My Best Treasures

My special treasure to me . . .
Is my signed football because
It reminds me of all the good times.

My special treasure to me . . .
Is my family and friends
Because they play with me.

My special treasure to me . . .
Is my pool table
With a hundred games in it.

My special treasures to me . . .
Are my trophies
Because they remind me of playing
For Predators Under-Eights.

Cory King (8)
Bishop Tufnell Junior School

My Diamond

In the deep, deep sea
There's a dark, dark cave
Where the shiny diamonds live
As glittering as the stars
As precious as a lock of hair
Shiny as gold
It is as rough as wood
Oh, what a beautiful diamond!

Alexander Trouchkin (8)
Bishop Tufnell Junior School

My Treasure

A crown like fabulous gold
A sword as priceless as a crystal
A dagger like bronze.

A turquoise ring as precious as dazzling gold
A ruby like a silver platter ring
A flagon like crystal gold.

A gold bar like diamond gold
A gold-plated earring like a gold jet
A blood-red ruby like a fiery sunset.

Iain Lacey (8)
Bishop Tufnell Junior School

Hidden Treasure

My hidden treasures are
My mum and dad
Because they are my family
My pets also
Because they make me laugh

I found a beautiful rock
Like an eye
It had all the detailed veins on it

I will keep it for my life
Then pass it onto my children.

Sean Gale (8)
Bishop Tufnell Junior School

Squirrel's Hidden Treasure

In my garden I sometimes see,
A squirrel playing in the rain,
He jumps across from tree to tree,
Rushes down and up again.

The squirrel stops and suddenly sees,
An empty bird feeder on a branch,
A buzzing sound from a bee,
Came swooping to a plant.

Oh no! The nuts have gone,
And it's time to eat,
I need to hunt for nutty treasure,
I'll have to hide and seek.

He sees his friend digging,
And looking all around,
He hides and waits,
Not making any sound.

When his friend has gone,
He rushes to the spot,
Digs up all the treasure,
And eats up all the lot.

Hooray!

Gemma Ward (9)
Chesworth Junior School

What Do I See?

As I walk along the sandy beach
Glistening stars come from the caves.
Rubbish washed ashore from the strength of the waves.
I stop, I stare, I wonder, should I dare?
I step into the mouth of the cave,
I will be brave.

Slowly, I move the rubbish away,
Something sparkles my way.
Behind a rock a crystal I find,
Its colour so bright it dazzles my mind.
I cover it up and bury it deep.
I go home and dream about it in my sleep.

Harry Roadley (10)
Chesworth Junior School

Hidden Treasure

The submarine is going down,
Going down, going down.

A jellyfish jiggles.

The submarine is going down,
Going down, going down.

The seaweed squiggles.
Where is the treasure?

There's an old shipwreck,
Could the treasure be in there?

There's a shark,
Maybe it's guarding the golden cross.

Rusty old swords are lying in the wreck,
A glint of shining gold.

And there it is - the golden cross,
Lined with jewels, treasure chests around.

But I will leave it
In its sandy bed
Forever.

Ryan Owner (9)
Chesworth Junior School

Treasure Well Hidden

He knew she had beautiful diamonds,
He had seen her wearing them,
He thought he would steal them for himself,
And get lots of money for them.

He found his torch and his skeleton key,
Dressed in black from head to toe,
He went to her house in the middle of the night,
And went to have a go.

It was quiet and dark when he got there,
He knew how to kill the alarm,
He went in quickly and started to search
In room after room after room.

He looked in the cupboards, the drawers and the safe,
Behind the pictures on the wall,
Under the floorboards and in every box,
He couldn't find them anywhere at all.

On the way out he stepped on the cat,
And the screech woke her up in a fright,
She put on her dressing gown and got out of bed,
And nervously put on the light.

She saw what a mess the burglar had left,
And quickly she phoned 999,
Before the big, fat policeman arrived,
She knew that her diamonds were fine.

She laughed as she looked at her glass chandelier,
And said, 'I was clever to hide them in here.'

Joe Lucas (10)
Chesworth Junior School

Little Treasures

Out of my open window
On a summer's night,
I see the little spirits
All in the moonlight.

Oh! I believe, I believe, I believe.

All in spider-silk dresses
Out on the warm night air,
Dancing, laughing, chattering
I wish I was there.

Oh! I believe, I believe, I believe.

They are all about to dance
In their special ring,
'Hark! What is that gentle sound
That makes their ears go ting-a-ling?'

Oh! I believe, I believe, I believe.

'Tis the tomcat, they say
We must go and run,
Fly up to the child's window,
Fly up, up and away.

Oh! I believe, I believe, I believe.

All the beautiful fairies are dancing with me,
It's joyous, it's wonderful and magical too.
There's no doubt about it,
It's definitely true!

Camilla Patel (10)
Chesworth Junior School

The Book Of The Dead

I was in Hamunaptra, Egypt
Reading hieroglyphic translations:
'He who enters this temple
Shall suffer a painful death in waiting!'

I ignored this completely
And walked in with anticipation
Suddenly, I heard a distant sound
I knew this was a no good vacation.

I found a giant cartouche on a wall
I couldn't find out what it meant
I looked a little closer
Then water spurted out of a dent!

I turned around full of worry
I was now totally wet
And at the distant door
Was something I'd never met!

It was a decomposing mummy!
It was carrying the Book of the Dead!
It threw it at me, I hit the wall
The mummy was now over my head!

It moved closer to me, I rolled out of the way
It kicked down the cartouche from the wall
It sprinted at me, his foot caught a rock
And it leapt into a face-flat fall!

I grabbed the book and ran for my life
Hoping the mummy wouldn't attack
I dashed out the temple, got on my camel
Daring not to look back.

I thought of happiness as my camel fled
I can't believe it's the Book of the Dead!

Chris Mason (10)
Chesworth Junior School

HIDDEN TREASURES

In the morning when I wake up
My fluffy, black kitten jumps on my bed
I don't really mind
Then she licks my face
But I don't mind.

So I get up and get dressed,
My kitten follows me down the stairs
And she tries to climb up my leg,
But she rarely makes it, only sometimes.

When I have my breakfast,
She sits on my feet,
She looks at me with her sea-blue eyes,
Waiting for her breakfast.

I have to go to school now, I tell her,
That I have to leave her alone, I'll soon be back.
But I have to find her when I get home from school,
Sometimes I find her and sometimes I don't,
I will never know where she will hide next.

That is why she is a hidden treasure.

Rebecca Neale (10)
Chesworth Junior School

Hidden Treasures

It was hot and gloomy in the Valley of the Kings
When I first unearthed this glorious treasure
I'd worked long and hard for weeks and weeks
To try and discover a lifelong ambition.

It was a wonderful sight seeing those beautiful things
So I called down my men to dig them out
We worked all day and night in the dust and heat
And then discovered to our amazement
A golden sarcophagus shimmering with Nubian gems.

We all stood in wonder and thought what lay beneath
The mysteries of ancient times gone by
With excitement and fear we searched on
In anticipation more gold could be found.

Hidden within the tomb
We unearthed a stack of papyrus scrolls
Secrets to be told
By the light of the moon we lifted our treasures
Into the cold night air.

To Cairo we went, to the museum
Where everybody could see my discovery
So Pharaoh Akhenaten and his treasure
Will be seen forever and ever.

Dean Little (11)
Chesworth Junior School

Bird's Treasure

In the garden on the ground
there are many treasures to be found.
Twigs for a nest
and worms to eat
lying near my little feet.

Up in the tree, high in the sky
two little eggs in my nest lie -
golden and round
never to be found.

Francesca McDowell (8)
Chesworth Junior School

ME AND TED'S FIRST TREASURE HUNT

When the moon shines and all is quiet,
My ted and I are asleep.
The morning comes and I awake,
Then my teddy does the same.
We jump out of bed with lazy heads
And get ready for the day.
Then suddenly I remember,
It's now the month of *May!*
Out of our room, in for a wash,
Down the stairs and on with the clothes.
Run down the hallway,
Out of the door,
Through the gate - and into spring.
We're walking, we're talking,
We're still not there.
We arrive at Barrack fields,
'But where is Denne Hill?
Oh look you silly bear, it's just over there!'
My bear and I walk through the meadow
And meet our friends, filled with good news.
So we followed them round the great oak tree.

Where we find . . .
A new lamb being born!

Beth Mae MacDonald (8)
Chesworth Junior School

Hidden Treasures

My grandad is special
He is a star in the sky
Gold, silver and shiny and bright
He is kind and gentle
I miss him so much
Grandad is the treasure I can't touch
He is hidden in a star
The diamond in the night which was flashing in my window
Grandad I wish you didn't go
And never left me alone.

Ray Allen (9)
Chesworth Junior School

My Mum's Hidden Treasures

1, 2, 3, 4, 5
6, 7, 8, 9, 10
Ready or not
Here I come
Are you here?
Are you there?
Are you anywhere?
Under the table,
Under the chair,
Anywhere?
Anyone here?
Anyone there?
Anyone under there?

Found you!

Benn McIntyre (9)
Chesworth Junior School

My Grandad, My Treasure

My grandad was tall
He also played football.

My grandad played tennis
And was sometimes a menace.

My grandad made models
But hey, no dolls.

My grandad liked taking photographs
And always made me laugh.

My grandad fished
And always wished.

My grandad sometimes went walking
And never stopped talking.

My grandad liked to snooze
But he never touched the booze.

My grandad
My treasure.

Arran Lindgren (7)
Chesworth Junior School

Caves

Snow leopards snug and warm in their den
Miners picking away at rock, searching for gold
Bears caring for their young away in their den
A dragon tucked away at the back of a cave
A flood gushing through a mine hole
An Egyptian tomb with mummies and ruins.

Liam Coughlan (9)
Chesworth Junior School

The Pirates' Treasure

Our hidden treasure
Is our pleasure
We demand
For our command
To dig up our hidden treasure.

Our hidden treasure is in a chest
It's as big as one man's breast
We bet
And will get
Our hidden treasure.

Our hidden treasure is hard to find
It's difficult to work out whether it's in front or behind
We'll find the treasure whatever bars the way
Even if we have to drag the bay
We'll find our hidden treasure.

We've found our hidden treasure and we'll all get our share
And we challenge you to take some if you dare
But you will get nowhere
But under the foot of a bear
But we now have the hidden treasure.

David Rowland (10)
Chesworth Junior School

Treasure Is . . .

Treasure is a big, fat teddy bear lying on your bed
Treasure is a vast, long sausage sizzling in the pan
Treasure is a best friend cracking a joke
Treasure is a lovely memory bouncing in your head

Treasure is a prized photograph propped against a wall
Treasure is a shining shell sleeping on the shore
Treasure is your favourite drink silently sitting in your hand
Treasure is a golden laugh echoing in the wind.

Ciaran Macklin (9)
Chesworth Junior School

TURTLES

A turtle waddles cautiously
Along the sandy shore,
To lay her eggs and leave them there
Alone forever more.

The treasures lie beneath the sand
Inside their leathery shells,
What time of day or where they are
They really cannot tell.

The eggs are hatching slowly
There's a hundred if not more,
They now begin their journey
To the waves at the seashore.

Predators are waiting,
For the turtles to appear,
They peck and grab the babies
As they scurry far and near.

Sadly only twenty-two
Reach the sea and swim away,
Spending years and growing large
To return another day.

Victoria Paterson (9)
Chesworth Junior School

EVERYONE HAS A TREASURE

Everyone has a treasure,
a treasure big or small.

Everyone has a treasure,
a treasure above them all.

Everyone has a treasure,
to keep them nice all day.

Everyone has a treasure,
but sometimes they won't say.

I have a treasure,
a treasure that's quite small.

Without this small treasure,
I wouldn't be at all.

That treasure is my family,
they are a treasure and nothing else.

David Nicholas (11)
Chesworth Junior School

RUBY RED

The light sparkles on the red jewels
And the golden brooch shines bright
Many bold coloured gems reflecting light
Dancing, prancing, flickering pools.

The shining shadows from a silver chest
A richness in all their shines
In the midnight sky their clear outlines
But one shone out from all the rest.

Peeking out from a pearly bed
The giant diamond shimmered
And all the others brightly glimmered
But there is nothing that shines like the ruby red!

Nathan Taylor (8)
Chesworth Junior School

What Will I Get For Christmas?

Could it be the skateboard hiding over there?
I can see the Christmas paper leaning on the chair.
Maybe there's some make-up hiding in those boxes.
Ooh, mummies can be sly sometimes,
Just like wild foxes.
I looked under Mummy's bed last night,
To see what I could find,
But Mum, she caught me out
And said I was unkind.

I wish I could be patient,
And wait for Christmas Day,
But I get so excited,
It seems a long time away.

Christmas Day is here at last,
The big day has arrived,
The Christmas tree's surrounded,
By boxes fat and wide.

But how could she have hidden these things,
That I can't decide.
I look at Mum with gleaming eyes,
But all she does is smile.

Stacey Cattermole (10)
Chesworth Junior School

Hidden Treasures

I wake up on a sunny morning
and I go to see my friends.
We are going treasure hunting
to see what we can find.

We get into our boat
and go out to sea.
We stop the boat and jump in
to see what we can see.

We find an old ship
so we start to look around.
Then we spot a box and open it
a bag of gold we find.

The gold is shining very brightly
so we take it back to our boat.
Then off we go back home
to show what we have found.

Aaron Peacock (8)
Chesworth Junior School

Hidden Treasure

Endless night
Like a big black curtain
Fairy lights twinkling - the stars
Drawn into a black hole
Planets swirling past
An undiscovered world
A hidden treasure.

Jordan Moores (9)
Chesworth Junior School

Seeds

Hidden treasures are:
Seeds popping out of the ground
All over the place
Here, there and everywhere.

In a few months
Some will become flowers
Some will become vegetables.

When you pull carrots
You need to be so careful
Because the tops might come off.

Some you dig right out of the ground
Be careful!
Don't chop off the roots!

Some treasure you pull off trees, bushes and plants
Some treasures are big, some small and some huge
Some even funny-shaped!

Ben Coughlan (8)
Chesworth Junior School

Hidden Treasure

I dream of finding one hundred gold keys
I dream of finding a thousand golden honeybees
I dream of finding my teddy bear
So I can give some loving care
I dream of finding a shimmering crown
That will go with my long, golden gown
Oh, if only I could find some *hidden treasure.*

Abigail Collins (10)
Chesworth Junior School

My Journey

I am going on a treasure hunt
To hunt for glorious gold
To steal from the powerful pirates.

I get my flag and start to make my boat
I get some Lego bricks to make some steps
To climb into my ship.

I replace the books in my book bag with a drink and a cookie
I tell my mum I'll be back by teatime
I step into my cardboard box boat
Anchors away!

Jack West (9)
Chesworth Junior School

Dragon Treasure

Hidden away in the side of a mountain
is a wealth beyond compare,
because this mountainside
is a dragon's lair.

In this mound
of gold and jewels,
are memories from
long gone duels.

At the end of this treacherous lair,
there is a dragon's egg
and a mother dragon taking care.

Michael McGearty (8)
Chesworth Junior School

The Poem

The poem is a hidden treasure locked in my mind
The truth will not break out before my eyes
A poem is the difficulty of my life
Nothing makes sense in this gloomy confusion
The pain and agony of not knowing the poem
Surrounded in mystery, locked away forever.
I plead and beg for forgiveness
Feeble suggestions only anger me
Everywhere I go, nothing will stop
The poem has no mercy on me
My parents give me no more help now
As they can give me assistance no more
I am on my own now to suffer
The poem is still my quest
That I have not yet discovered
My hidden treasure is the poem.

David Phillips (10)
Chesworth Junior School

Hidden Treasures

A box buried in the ground
that everyone says can never be found
filled with jewels, golden jewels
diamonds, necklaces
but that is not just the hidden treasure
your mum, dad, sister
grandma, grandad
are hidden treasures too.

Kathie Harris (9)
Chesworth Junior School

Once I Was An Archaeologist

When I was an archaeologist
I toured all over the world
I went to Egypt
And travelled deep inside a pyramid
I found a sarcophagus
And had a peep inside
I saw the mummy!

I went under the waves in the North Sea
I found a shipwreck
We looked round and found
Ten skeletons and a huge treasure chest

I went to China
Walked along the Great Wall
By one of the stones I found a gold ring

I went for a dig in Africa
There was loads of pottery

I went to Stonehenge
I found a carving in one of the stones
It looked like a man

But I found I'm a better poet
Than an archaeologist
So that's why I'm here now writing for you.

Rachael Tester (9)
Chesworth Junior School

My Toy Rabbit

My rabbit is blue, yellow and white,
He goes to bed with me every single night.

One day I lost him and it gave me such a fright,
My dad helped me find him and that made me feel all right.

He'd been at McDonald's all by himself,
The manager found him and put him on a shelf.

I thought he was gone, lost forever,
He really is my little treasure.

Rachel Swansborough (8)
Chesworth Junior School

Me

My mum went into my room
and found all my toys scattered on the floor.
It was me!

My mum went into the bathroom
and found water splashed up the walls.
It was me!

My mum went to the shop
and when she got back there was a mess.
It was me!

My mum went into my wardrobe
it was untidy.
It was me!

My mum went into the garden
and found all the plants cut up.
It was me!

My mum came into my bedroom
and saw me asleep.
It was me!

I am her little treasure.

Paul Dennett (7)
Chesworth Junior School

Deep Blue Sea

Far, far away,
There's a deep, blue sea.
The crystal-clear water with a shimmer in the mild waves,
Of the deep, blue sea.
In that deep, blue sea
Lies a big, old, brown, wooden ship.
A ship that sank to the bottom of the deep, blue sea,
A long time ago.
Two bones crossed over,
Above them, a big, big skull on the front of the big, brown ship.
The ship was a pirates' ship with hidden treasure.
Many went to the deep, blue sea,
In search of the hidden treasure,
Where the big, blue sapphire diamonds were said to live,
Somewhere in the deep, blue sea.
Never was the treasure found
In the deep, blue sea.
Strange, if only they looked closely
At the eyes of the big skull
On the front of the big, brown ship in the deep, blue sea.

Tasnima Ahmed (8)
Chesworth Junior School

My Best Friend

My best friend looks after me when I hurt myself
She cares and plays with me all day
She is really funny and plays jokes on me all the time
She gives me gifts of necklaces, bracelets and toy horses too
Best friends should be treasured
I am glad I have her for a friend.

Hannah Oakes (7)
Chesworth Junior School

HIDDEN TREASURE

I sit under the tree,
it's autumn and the red-gold leaves are falling.
Suddenly, I don't know why, my hand clasps an acorn
I softly cradle it in my hand, it's no longer than my thumb joint,
it is smooth to touch, almost silky.
I look up at the tree, a massive trunk,
huge, impregnable bastions rising, soaring,
gargantuan boughs curving across the sky in huge waves,
they seem to be soaring above me.
Nimble and slender twigs almost touching the heavens above me,
how could such a mighty tree have grown from such a minute acorn?
How could such an indestructible monster have grown from such a tiny treasure, the treasure hidden in that acorn?
The leaves glow red, burning with an eerie light,
the light of the setting sun, it's so beautiful.
Now I have to go, I take the acorn, I will plant it and it will grow,
maybe I will have an oak tree.

Daniel McArthur (10)
Chesworth Junior School

A HIDDEN TREASURE OUT OF THIS WORLD

My hidden treasure has a loving pumping heart
Two arms to hug me when I am feeling down
Two legs to play games with me
Two brown eyes to watch me in the night to make sure I'm safe
And two ears to listen to me
My hidden treasure is my mum!

Luke Gooch (11)
Chesworth Junior School

Hidden Treasures

Search up high and search down low,
look for the hidden treasures below.

My cuddly rabbit who's there for me,
when I'm feeling sad.

My mum who always does her best,
even when she's mad.

Hidden treasures.
Hidden treasures.

My youngest cousin, she's only three,
she makes me glad, glad, glad.

My books, I'm forever reading them,
they're my latest fad.

Hidden treasures.
Hidden treasures.

My summer hols' diaries,
oh, what fun we had.

My house, my home, my family,
they're really not half bad!

Hannah Harris (11)
Chesworth Junior School

Sunken Treasures

In olden days there were pirates bold
Who often sank other boats loaded with glorious gold
Now people dive to the ocean's floor
They find gold, treasures and more.

They sell the treasures and the gold
And have piles of money when it all is sold.
They buy new stuff, but it won't last
Not like the sunken treasures from the past.

Peter Morgan (9)
Chesworth Junior School

Hidden Treasure

You never know
What you might find in a library.
For a library is full of hidden treasures,
Fascinating things to learn and read.
One can study about music,
Poetry, rhythm or rhyme.
Amongst the hidden treasures you can explore:
The wonders of the world, words of wisdom,
Even how to read minds.
In fact, you can even learn to fly!
Why, you can escape into your hidden treasure
By going back in time,
History all around you in the library.
We can go back to Roman times
To kings and castles and ancient kingdoms,
Visit many battlefields from times gone by.
I can read about the wild, wild west and imagine I'm
walking with Red Indians,
Sleeping under the stars with wolves.
So you see,
Hidden treasures can be found so near to home,
Just down at the library.

Charlotte Croft (10)
Chesworth Junior School

Hidden Treasures

One morning I saw some paper,
Sticking out from under a rock.
It seemed to be a treasure map,
With a key for a golden lock.

I looked hard at the map,
And when the time was right,
I followed the directions,
Until it was late at night.

The next morning came,
So I searched across the sand.
That's when I met the mermaid,
Reaching out her hand.

We dived right down,
Under the deep blue sea.
What do you think I found?
A treasure chest for the key.

I opened up the magic box,
With hidden treasure inside.
The golden jewels were sparkling,
Beautiful and shimmering under the tide.

The mermaid swam with the chest,
Straight back to the beach.
I turned around to say 'Goodbye'
But she'd vanished without a peep.

Amber Verrall (10)
Chesworth Junior School

Hidden Treasures

Diving deep down,
Gliding through the inky darkness,
Through seaweed blue and green,
A shipwreck lying on the seabed,
I swim closer.

A treasure chest,
Lying on the coral sand,
Treasures spilling out,
I swim closer, closer,
A shark guards the treasure
Glides away,
Skeletons lying in the sand,
Closer, closer, I look inside.

So much treasure,
Diamonds, sovereigns and glistening gold,
Old gold coins,
Treasures of the deep.

Old gold,
Forgotten treasure
Of many years gone by,
Lying in the sand,
Lying hidden in the sea.

Gemma Vizor (11)
Chesworth Junior School

Hidden Treasures

There was a little rabbit,
Who sailed across the sea,
He wore a light blue jacket,
Just like me.

I think he's looking for treasure,
Lots and lots of gold,
He has already got lots,
Now all the shops are sold.

If you look very carefully,
You can see him putting on his suit,
I hate to say this,
But he looks very cute.

He's getting in the water,
I think he's going to drown,
First you see him swimming,
Then he's going down.

All he sees are fishes,
Then it starts getting bright,
He starts getting a chill,
And starts getting a fright.

Then he realises it's a chest,
Filled with gold,
He tries to pick it up,
But it's impossible to hold.

Then he sees a shark,
With sharp teeth,
Then you find you're in his mouth,
He thinks you're his beef.

Lee Kiely (9)
Chesworth Junior School

JOLLY ROGER'S TREASURE

Long ago a story was told,
Of pirates' treasure, a casket of gold,
Buried in sand far, far away,
In a hot, sunny place called Cut Throat Bay.

The crew and I have set to sea,
Already we have a map and key,
We have directions we have to follow,
All the way to Shipmate's Hollow.

We arrive at last and look around,
High and low for the 'X' on the ground,
The old, crooked tree points to the spot,
Where the 'X' is marked under Hangman's Knot.

We get out the spades and start to dig,
Then we hit something quite big,
A big, brown casket with a lock that was rusted,
Lucky for us, the lock is busted!

We open the lid and look inside,
The men and I can't believe our eyes,
The casket is full of lovely things,
Rubies and pearls, and large, gold diamond rings.

We set sail home to return to our wives,
Knowing the treasure will change our lives,
We all know that we will have much pleasure,
Thanks to Old Jolly Roger's treasure.

Kieran Greig (11)
Chesworth Junior School

THE VOLCANO'S TREASURE

The volcano is deep and dark,
With tunnels that lead to a troll.
He is ugly and scary as a midnight storm,
And guards precious jewels and gold.

People who dare to enter
Will get a clonk on the head
And be thrown in the hot, sizzling lava,
Or maybe eaten instead.
Don't bother the troll, he's too greedy to share,
Go and look for your treasure elsewhere!

Christopher Morgan (7)
Chesworth Junior School

TREASURE ON THE BEACH

One day we went to our caravan,
The weather was not very good,
So we set off to the beach,
To see if the sea was calm.

We took our metal detector,
And we went for a walk along the beach,
Passing the detector over the pebbles
To see if it made a sound.

All of a sudden the bleep went off,
So we bent down and started to dig.
The hole got bigger and bigger,
Then we found it, it was a ring.

Nicholas Peacock (11)
Chesworth Junior School

Cocoon

A small leaf waiting on a branch,
The wind blows, but it does not fall,
The weeks pass, it shakes, but there is no wind.

For it is a cocoon,
Waiting on a branch,
Shaking from time to time,
More weeks pass,
But not a sign of what is inside.

All of a sudden I see something,
A little antenna,
Then a body with folded up wings,
The wings open,
Upon the wings lay a beautiful array
Of bright colours shining in the sunlight,
With a flitter and a flutter, away it flies,
Leaving the empty cocoon behind.

Emma Anscomb (10)
Chesworth Junior School

Sandy Beach

A stranded island in the middle of the sea,
Coconuts hanging from a palm tree.

The golden sand sparkling away,
A golden eagle catching its prey.

The sandy beach still lies there,
But who knows where?

Gemma Fry (10)
Chesworth Junior School

The Silent Galleon

Deep in the darkened ocean,
Where the seabed is a junkyard.
The galleon lies still,
Silent,
Never moving an inch.

Divers dive to the galleon,
To seek the hidden treasure.
Who is guarding it?
A great white shark,
A shark with razor-sharp teeth.

Divers grab the old treasure chest.
The jaws of the shark snap.
Snap!
They have the treasure,
The shark is cheated,
His dinner is gone.

Rising divers celebrate.

Shaun Denman (10)
Chesworth Junior School

Treasure

From all the hours of leisure spent looking for treasure
My feet are covered in blisters
But now I realise that whatever I find
Won't be as precious to me
As my two little twin sisters.

Glenn Smith (9)
Chesworth Junior School

My Beloved . . .

Salty tears, the shocked expression.
Not believing, it can't be true!
Worried thoughts buzzing around my puzzled mind.
It's just a bump, changing everything.
No longer the youngest.
Me, an older sister.
But it soon grew larger.
It became more precious to me.
The anticipation of her birth.
It's a girl!
It's a real person.
So delicate.
Visiting the hospital nearly every day.
At home, I wait for her arrival.
Stomach whirling, swirling.
She's home, and soon her warm body is in my arms.
My darling little sister.
Watching her grow.
Her first smile.
Making her laugh.
Her innocent chuckle.
So here I am.
Doubtful no longer.
Writing a poem.
About little Isabel.
My hidden treasure.

Juliet Harris (11)
Chesworth Junior School

A Hidden Treasure

Searching for stalactites,
Dangling from the cave,
Seeing beautiful crystals,
But still no sign of stalactites,
Getting gloomier every step,
But still not finding our reason here,
Searching every gap,
Needing to turn the torch on,
Such prize sat in front of us,
Glistening gold for a border,
Getting closer and excited,
I touched the box and tried the lid,
Then we burst with excitement,
As I opened the treasure,
About a million diamonds,
Stare at me,
Shining with royalty,
All of a sudden we ran to the surface,
Carrying our hidden treasure.

Emily Barrell (10)
Chesworth Junior School

Hidden Treasures

Winter's here, the clouds are grey,
I lie in bed wishing for a summer's day,
The world looks bad, cold and dark,
The trees look lonely in the park.
A month goes by, still feeling cold,
Spring's coming soon as we are told.

I look out of the window expecting the same dreary scene,
But instead I see a world that's green.
Am I dreaming?
The trees have leaves,
The bulbs have shoots,
Will I find another hidden treasure?
If I do, it will be a pleasure!

Mollie Wilkins (10)
Chesworth Junior School

The Boy Who Struck Gold

There was a boy called Andy,
Who found an empty bottle of brandy.

When opening the lid,
There was hid . . .

A mysterious map rolled up tightly,
With a piece of ribbon wrapped round it lightly.

He sat down slowly on the sand,
And stared at the map in his hand.

He got up with pleasure,
To realise there was treasure.

He met a man called Dave,
Who showed him the way to the cave.

He went inside and found a spade,
And stood by the hole which he had made.

As he began to get cold,
He suddenly realised he had struck gold.

Craig Potter (10)
Chesworth Junior School

I HAVE A TREASURE

I have a treasure,
A treasure hidden deep.
I have a treasure,
No one can peep.
I have a treasure,
A treasure hidden well.

I have a treasure,
So nobody can tell.
I have a treasure,
A treasure inside me.
I have a treasure,
What can it be?
I have a treasure,
A treasure from the start.
I'll tell you my treasure,
It is my heart.

Darren Cattermole (11)
Chesworth Junior School

BEST FRIEND

B est friend
E very day
S mile always
T rue as she can be

F un in different ways
R unning with me
I listen to her chattering
E very word means a lot to me
N o one could replace her!
D iamond, she's a true gem.

Rachel Banks (10)
Chesworth Junior School

Memories

Special memories whirling in my mind,
Christmas, birthdays and pleasurable times,
Days out and holidays of all kinds,
A photograph in a drawer, that we find.

Helping in the garden, planting seeds,
And him giving me anything I need,
Walking the dog across the fields and far away,
I loved to see him every day.

When I think of him, I feel so sad,
Because of all the great times that we had,
He was one special man, my grandad.

Rebecca Nash (11)
Chesworth Junior School

Hidden Treasures

In the middle of the volcano,
it bubbles hot and sticky,
it is waiting to burst out from here
steaming red and pretty.

The pressure is getting stronger,
it's building up and up,
it's getting hotter and wants to go,
and is ready to erupt.

It's flowing down the mountain,
with shining molten rock,
the lava is burning trees and grass,
it's a race against the clock.

Thomas West (10)
Chesworth Junior School

My Treasures

In my life there are two things that are very important.
My mum and dad are things, I call them my treasure.

They help me out with anything, I only have to ask,
It may be cleaning football boots, *yuk!* Or ironing my clothes.

It may be giving me a lift to a club and picking me up when
it's finished.
When I get home there will always be a cup of cocoa waiting.

Day in, day out, they put up with me, however naughty I have been.
Don't get me wrong, I get told off if they feel the need!

My mum stays at home and looks after us, my dad earns our keep.
I will always be grateful to them for making my life so sweet.

Our house is happy and mad but I'm so glad that my life contains
Such fantastic treasures.

Ryan Laker (10)
Chesworth Junior School

Hidden Treasure Under The Sea

Under the sea,
Under the sea,
Where the treasure lies
Beside the Titanic's ancient side
Under the sea.

Red gems, blue gems,
Green gems, yellow gems.
What a magnificent sight
Found in the shipwreck
Under the sea.

Old pirates' bones left from years ago
Lying all over the seabed.
Some buried, some broken,
Some washed away,
Under the sea.

Dolphins diving into the stormy sea,
Looking for the treasure.
They pop in and out of the water.
Under the sea,
Under the sea.

Everard Payne (10)
Chesworth Junior School

HIDDEN TREASURE

A hidden treasure,
what could it be?
Something gleaming deep under the sea.

A hidden treasure,
a radiant face,
or a sacred, special place.

A hidden treasure,
your best friend,
someone on whom you can always depend.

A hidden treasure,
a small little seed,
will grow into a thing of beauty if you give the care it needs.

A hidden treasure,
this poem I write?
Which I hope you have read with delight!

Stephanie Barr (11)
Chesworth Junior School

TREASURE IS EVERYWHERE!

Treasure is everywhere
It's hiding under the sea,
Treasure is everywhere
It's inside you and me

Treasure is anywhere
It's somewhere in a cave,
Treasure is anywhere
It's maybe something you crave

Treasure is anything
It might be your teddy bear,
Treasure is anything
It might be your mum's love and care

Treasure is touchable
It's hovering around you
Treasure is untouchable
It could be something you do

Treasure is far away
It may be out of reach
Treasure is far away
At the other end of the beach

Treasure is nearby
It's floating through the air
Treasure is nearby
All you have to do is care!

Matthew M Davies (11)
Chesworth Junior School

HIDDEN TREASURES

Down at the bottom of the sea,
where the fishes sip their tea.

The treasure is hidden, hidden, hidden.

Under the shimmering pink coral,
The sea creatures tell the moral.

The treasure is hidden, hidden, hidden.

In the chest of gold and silver,
There's a map written by Sir Chilver.

The treasure is hidden, hidden, hidden.

Every fish digs and digs,
But all they find are twigs.

The treasure is hidden, hidden, hidden.

One day will the treasure be free
From its place beneath the sea?

The treasure is hidden, hidden, hidden.

Sunlight beams, shining down
Through the waters, dark and green.
Down, down, deep to the spot where
Just a glimmer of the chest can be seen.

The treasure is hidden, hidden, hidden.

For a thousand years the golden chest of plunder,
Lay silent, the beautiful jewels and gems a-wonder.

The treasure is hidden, hidden, hidden.

Lauren Harding (10)
Chesworth Junior School

My Journey

I had finally got here at last.
I had gone through the most daring and dangerous tasks.
I had gone over black and burning coals that were steaming hot.
I was finally here where 'X' marks the spot.
I had swung over crocodiles' snapping jaws.
I ran away from a tiger's slashing paws.
I dodged a deadly cobra snake.
I just managed to avoid an earthquake.
I sailed the Norwegian Sea.
I had climbed the tallest and toughest trees.
I had fought the most powerful beasts.
I had been rewarded by holy priests.
I was now looking for gold.
I had to dig, I was told.
Slowly I was digging and suddenly I saw the chest.
When I looked inside, I thought, this is the best.

Sara Powell (9)
Chesworth Junior School

Atom Treasures

The atom is a world of treasures
Which are so beautiful.
They are a 'must see'.
The electrons orbit the nucleus
Like moons round a planet.
Inside the nucleus, there are two
Types of nucleons you'll find.
The proton is positively charged.
(The electron's negative.)

The neutron has no charge.
Inside each nucleon there are
Three amazing little quarks.
So that's my talk finished.
Hope you enjoyed it!
(And one final note -
Don't destroy atoms!)

Alice Broadribb (9)
Chesworth Junior School

THE VIKING HORDE

In a dark, gloomy tunnel,
Deep under the ground,
A team of archaeologists work,
What is this?
A glint of gold,
Scraping gently, the workers dig and dig.

A silver cup is shimmering in the bright new sunlight,
One wrinkly hand tugs carefully at the first shiny find,
Another scrape and a golden sword slowly appears,
Thick rubber gloves slide the sword out of its ancient position,
As it is raised, tiny jewels sparkle.

The sunlight fades slowly away as the workers pack their bags,
Only two items were uncovered that very long day,
Who knows what lies beneath the thick earth?

Patrick Harris (9)
Chesworth Junior School

It Was A Moonlit Night

It was a moonlit night as I looked across the sea,
And in the distance was my destiny.

We sat around the fire watching the pirates approach,
I knew our treasure was in danger or it was what they wished to poach.

'Prepare the ship for dock,' I heard the captain cry,
He was extremely full of excitement and I knew exactly why.

The treasure is safely hidden, we're ready for our fight,
We'll give it all we've got; we'll give it all our might.

The captain gave a signal to attack our pirates' foe.
The battle was over in a flash; they didn't get our dough.

Ashleigh Bayton (10)
Chesworth Junior School

Deep Sea Treasure

A sparkly crystal hidden deep,
Among winding weeds growing on a shipwreck,
The weeds dancing as the water ripples around them,
A crab scuttling by searching for food,
As it passes, it knocks a weed with its claws,
And the crystal rolls into the sand,
As a mermaid glides by, the crab scuttles away,
She sits herself on a rock and gazes into the mirror,
In the corner of the mirror, a little shining speck!
The mermaid swimming past the weeds,
Sees the crystal and picks it up,
She glides gracefully back to her cave,
Placing the crystal in a bed of seaweed,

A hidden treasure found forever!

Samantha Beckwith (10)
Chesworth Junior School

Gold Is Near, Pure And Clear

One sunny day I was at the beach,
I heard a rustle near,
I turned and saw a tattered paper.

Gold is near, pure and clear.

I read the paper, yellow and old,
To my delight it was a map.
Full of excitement I jumped in deep.

Gold is near, pure and clear.

The murky depths were the sight I saw,
The sand a metre away,
Then the glint,
The shimmer I was waiting for.

Gold is near, pure and clear.

I dug and shifted all the dirt,
And pulled out what I hoped was treasure.

Gold is near, pure and clear.

Once back on shore I sat and gazed,
At what I found below.
To my surprise it was a coin,
All shiny and golden like the sun up high.

Gold is near, pure and clear.

Natasha Little (9)
Chesworth Junior School

KENNING SNAKE

Scary creature
Scaly feature
Tongue hisser
Poisonous kisser
Tail shaker
Fear maker
Tummy glider
Back slider
Mouse killer
Tummy filler
Fast mover
Bunny hoover
Blood drinker
Cave slinker.

Georgina Brown (10)
East Wittering Primary School

KENNING GERBIL

Swift mover
Hates the hoover
Fast digger
Bad swimmer
High jumper
Quick runner
Stinging bite
Alive at night
Eats by day
Hides in hay.

Sophie Buckland (11)
East Wittering Primary School

Kenning Crocodile

Maneater
Fish beater
Sharp claws
Huge paws
Snappy mouth
Living south
Nostrils flair
Dangerous lair
Wild attacker
Train tracker
Enormous tail
Deadly trail.

Dominic Webster (11)
East Wittering Primary School

Kenning Tiger

Striped back
Orange and black
Pointed ears
Eats deers
Strong ripper
Fish dipper
Swift pouncer
Running bouncer
Sharp paws
Blood from jaws
Kills with claws.

Perry Willson (10)
East Wittering Primary School

The Tornado

Forming over the grassy plain
Starting its terrible reign
Moving quickly, it gains speed
Ravaging forests, it knocks down trees;
Destroying houses, it moves through town;
Absolutely terrifying, leaving nothing sound.

Heading for the forest,
Where lots of creatures live,
Devastating lots of homes,
Humans and animals alike
Destroying peace,
Causing utter chaos.

Continuing its journey,
Not stopping for anything,
Smashing things, sweeping away the wreckage,
Anything glass gets shattered,
Anything concrete gets smashed.

Reaching the forest,
It tears right through,
Smashing trees and crashing undergrowth,
Sending branches flying.
Twisting, turning, down its own path,
Flailing, thrashing, will it ever end?

Crossing the sea, the water spins,
Drips flying everywhere,
Hitting things with a salty sting,
Whisking up the water, creating a whirlpool.
Stunning the fish, ripping up seaweed,
The whirlpool now fully formed.

Arriving on the island, whirlpool died down,
Tornado preparing to do more damage,
Island life faces total annihilation,
All the trees: elimination.

Now it's slowing, calming down,
No more damage for it to cause
Once all-powerful,
Now no more than a gentle breeze.

Sebastian Green (11)
East Wittering Primary School

Kenning Elephant

Trumpet blower
Tree thrower
Trunk swinger
Tail flinger
Ear flapper
Mud slapper
Heavy mover
Slow groover
Big feet
Tusks meet
Eye roller
Dung bowler.

Rebecca Meloy (10)
East Wittering Primary School

KENNING BUTTERFLY

A colour flyer
A cocoon dyer
A pattern maker
An insect taker
An eye-catcher
A pretty catcher
A fly eater
A sky leaper.

Gemma Collins (11)
East Wittering Primary School

KENNING MONKEY

Crazy swinger
Fast runner
Fruit eater
Tree climber
Quiet listener
Flea eater
Tree sleeper.

Lauren Batson (10)
East Wittering Primary School

HAIKU - CLOUDS

Fluffy silkiness
Tender foggy fluff floats by
A smooth silver sponge.

Tiffany Merritt (10)
East Wittering Primary School

Kenning Tiger

Great leaper,
Stalking creeper,
Maneater,
Mean beater,
Bone crushing,
Runs rushing,
Sharp hearing,
Keeps sneering,
Sharp claws,
Giant jaws,
Huge paws.

Michael Chaloner (10)
East Wittering Primary School

Kenning - Parrot

Raisin raider
Magnificent mimicker
Perfect bomber
Beaked nutcracker
Colourful flyer
Fantastic flapper.

Matthew Sutcliff (10)
East Wittering Primary School

Haiku - Sadness

Silver tears dropping,
All alone in the darkness
Happiness needed.

Jodie Grigg (10)
East Wittering Primary School

KENNING LION

Gigantic claws
Hairy paws
Mean fighter
Enormous biter
Deer chaser
Lazy racer
High bouncer
Giant pouncer.

Martin Fuller (11)
East Wittering Primary School

KENNING SNAKE

Skin smooth
Quickly moves
Mice eater
Slimy weaver
Sneaking around
Along the ground
Tongue hisser
Body swisher.

Samantha Pannell (11)
East Wittering Primary School

HAIKU - BEACH

A surge of water.
Roar of water on the shore.
Moving reflection.

Miriam Callow (11)
East Wittering Primary School

Sun

Blazing, glistening, people sweat,
they squint as the sun gleams;
sun scorching the crispy plants;
sea reflecting like a mirror as the sun glistens;
animals dehydrating in the sultry sun;
sun peering round clouds and buildings.

Martin Stovell (10)
East Wittering Primary School

Wind

Gusts of wind suddenly blow up
And prickles of hair stand on end.
Now I hear howling,
Howling like a dog.
Wild, violent, raging gale,
Turning tornado, hurling hurricane,
Ripping down buildings,
Destroying lives.

Chloe Parker (11)
East Wittering Primary School

Spring

The sunflower is growing to the highest height.
Tall trees' leaves are sprouting with all their might.
Summer is coming hip, hip, hooray
And all the winter snow is going away.

Jack M Furlong
Great Ballard School

Me And My Pony

Me and my pony riding on the beach,
No smoky cars from the busy street.
People watching us ride, as my pony goes into a beautiful stride.
We go underwater to see the pretty fish
When I hear people shouting 'Let's have some liquorice!'
So I ride out of the water to see what's going on,
With my pony's mane blowing in the breeze,
Almost night I hope we don't freeze.
We are going away from the sea, let's go home and have some tea.

Bonita Forster (9)
Great Ballard School

Winter

Flowers are frosting up at night
The trees are frightened with fear
Snowflakes are drifting through the air
And Christmas is drawing near.

The frost is cold and icy
And the countryside misty and white
Yet children's happy faces
Set every street alight.

Fathers sleeping peacefully
By the fire, warm and bright
And dreams of magic fairies
Fill the children with delight.

Soon the morning sun awakes
The snowdrops lift their heads
Noises fill the streets again
And children leave their beds.

Catherine Knight (8)
Great Ballard School

Ladybird

The ladybird that
Seldom stops from climbing
All the day.

She climbs up
The rushes' tassel tops
Spreads her wings
And flies away.

Over the mountains
And far away
While her dangers sleep
She flies to her nest
Where she has
Her very wanted rest.

Felicity Holmes (8)
Great Ballard School

Football

I am round.
I like to be blown up tight.
I live in a net with all my brothers.
I want to be better than the others!
I hope the boys will choose me first.
Wa-hoo! It's me! Let's play footie!
I'm flying! I'm flying!
I'm zooming through the air.
The goalie missed me.
I'm in the net.
Goal!

William Wightman (9)
Great Walstead School

The Real Christmas

Christmas balls on Christmas trees,
Presents, toys, hope, excitement.
Is it really here again?

Stockings, turkey and Father Christmas
Are all part of our Christmas cheer.

But somehow far away,
Children lack opportunities we have today.
Starving, hungry, with lots of fear,
They don't have any Christmas cheers.

Sometimes I wish I could change the world,
And put a smile where there is pain.
Baby Jesus in a manger, come and bring joy again.

Josh Anderson (9)
Great Walstead School

Losing My Possessions

Wherever I go, whatever I do, whatever,
I leave something behind (not very clever).
Whether it's my coat, my money or my bag,
I always leave it behind, but then it's nag, nag *nag!*

How do I remember my stuff?
My mum's just had enough.
I shall have to pay for the things I've lost.
It's going to be an enormous cost.

How oh how do I remember?

Naomi Slater (9)
Great Walstead School

My Family

In my family there's my dad,
And his jokes are really bad.
My dad's cooking is a scare,
But it's not as bad as his hair.

In my family there's my mum,
Who always fills my empty tum.
She often picks me up from school,
And her jokes are really cool.

In my family there is Sam,
He really likes his home-made jam.
He is my naughty little brother,
Often winding up our mother.

In my family there is me,
I like scrambled eggs for tea.
All in all, we're not that bad,
Me and my brother, Mum and Dad.

Ben Johnson (9)
Great Walstead School

Anger Is Like . . .

Evil drilling into you,
Lightning hitting you
Drinking poison,
Being shot again and again,
A bomb waiting to go off,
A kettle boiling inside you,
Someone beating you,
Someone bullying you.

Benedict Smith (8)
Great Walstead School

HEREOS

My name is Hereos and my task is to row
In the trireme Eradicus - the ship that I know
My name is Hereos and my work is a strain
My back is breaking, my arms are in pain.

My name is Hereos - the war has begun
We are called into battle to make the foe run
My name Is Hereos - Eradicus is tough
The wind is wild and the water is rough

My name is Hereos - the enemy is near
The soldiers are shouting, but I have no fear
My name is Hereos - the Gods care for me well
The battle has ended, I am saved from my hell.

Charlie Wilkes (8)
Great Walstead School

THE LIFE OF THE FOX

A fox woke up
In a farm
He really was quite calm
Then he saw a bin
Boing he jumped right in
First he had something to eat
Then he went to sleep
He woke up forgetting it was morning
So he played around some grass until it was lunch
About halfway through a hunter came running
Run, run, run, run, run, run, run.

Jack Wrench (8)
Great Walstead School

Autumn

Leaves drifting round and round,
Soon they'll end up on the ground.
Different colours, yellow and red,
It's hard to imagine they are all dead.
Juicy apples green and red,
Corn is harvested for bread.
All the hedgehogs go to sleep,
Round the woods they no longer creep.
Squirrels store nuts underground,
Often they cannot be found.
Sparks from a bonfire dance and leap,
Guy Fawkes stands on a burning wood heap.
Fireworks bang and whistle and blow,
Soon people will kiss under mistletoe.
After autumn will come snow,
And fires in grates will softly glow.

Joshua Prince (9)
Great Walstead School

My Hobbies

Football crazy, chocolate mad,
Don't be lazy, don't be bad.

Ice cream sundaes, sherbet dips
Melting slowly on your lips.

Saturday, Sunday, school is out.
These are the days to dance and shout.

Holidays in the sun, swim in the sea,
These are the things that are fun to me.

William Wrench (10)
Great Walstead School

My Worst Nightmare

I had an awful dream
I woke up in a sweat
My heart was jumping up and down
And I had a massive frown

I dreamt there was no football
Not one piece of evidence in the land
For in my worst dream
Football had been banned

The stadiums had been demolished
The pitches all mangled up
Old people grew flowers
Where Maradona used his hand to win the World Cup

Then I remembered it was only a dream
My life was saved
Now that was a scream.

Kieran Lewis (10)
Great Walstead School

The Spaceship

The spaceship,
It zooms beyond this galaxy,
Fast, streamlined and dull,
Like a meteor,
It flies like a bird,
It makes me all excited,
Like an astronaut floating in the sky,
The spaceship,
Reminds us there are other planets out there.

Joy Martin (10)
Kingsham County Primary School

Glinting Glitter Ball

Glitter ball, glitter ball,
Glinting above me,
Twirling, whirling,
Shimmering, flickering,
Like a crazy disco diva
Dancing on the moon,
Like a golden medallion
Going round and round,
Making me feel
Dazzled and amazed,
Like I'm the Queen
Of the dance floor,
Glitter ball, glitter ball,
The light of the world?

Chloe Marchant (11)
Kingsham County Primary School

The Town Clock

The town clock
Has revolving hands
Staring, tall and still,
Like a wise old owl
Like a giant asleep on the spot
I feel satisfied to see the time,
I feel that it's a statue I rely on
The town clock
It's the leader I trust.

David Turner (11)
Kingsham County Primary School

THE ROSE

A single purple rose grows
in a shabby pot placed in the shade.
It looks sad and deserted,
like a bird trapped in a cage
gazing at the blue sky.
The lack of light leaves it
delicate like a spider's web.
A soft wind blows and the rose
loses its petals as they drift
to the ground like sycamore seeds,
it also has lost the elegant jewel
that gave it hope.
Who will notice it now?

Claire Shields (9)
Kingsham County Primary School

LIFE IN SPACE

Travelling through the universe
Seeing different things
Landing on every planet
Each one at a time
Looking for other creatures
Pink, purple and blue
Landing on Jupiter and Mars
Putting flags on all the stars
We have done what we came to do
To walk on many different places
Than the one we all know
That is Earth.

Liam Williams (11)
Kingsham County Primary School

The Silver Swan

She glides, she flies,
The sun sets, the water falls.
She starts at the beginning.

Out on the path people are talking,
She skids away still hearing the noise
Of the children screaming.

Now there are the bins being emptied
Into the river, she ducked out of the way.
She could just hear the other swans.

She followed the noise which led her
To the other swans,
The silver swan.

Rachael Bailey (9)
Kingsham County Primary School

The Butterfly

The butterfly,
The multicoloured caterpillar,
Flitter, flutter, flutter,
As colourful as a rainbow,
And as pretty as a Catherine wheel,
It makes me feel happy,
Now it can be free at last,
The butterfly,
It has now changed from a boring caterpillar,
To a stunning butterfly.

Priya Srirajan (11)
Kingsham County Primary School

It Isn't A Spirit, Is It? It Can't Be!

A spirit drifts in the creepy darkness
Of this cold, silent, deserted corridor,
Leading into my clean, clear scary front room
And can anyone seek what he's trying to discover?
Wailing with the noise of the howling wind.
It isn't a spirit, it can't be, you whisper to yourself.
Staring over the frosty window sill,
But the world around is quiet and deathly still.

As the spirit glides by outside the warmth of the room,
A cold, ghostly glimmering fills the gloom
And filters through your half-closed door
Filling your brain with doubts once again.
It isn't a spirit, is it? It can't be.
Going carefully outside to turn off the dull light,
But the passageway is black like the dark, gloomy night.

Kristie Clarke (10)
Kingsham County Primary School

The Golden Snitch

The golden snitch
Faster than the speed of light,
Zooming, darting, gliding,
Like a golfball dashing through the sky,
Like a shooting star glinting in the fine night,
It makes me feel I'm the Quidditch Queen,
Like I've won the cup and accomplished the tournament,
The golden snitch
Reminds us how reading helps the imagination!

Heidi Pointet (10)
Kingsham County Primary School

A Summer's Day

I saw a flower bloom from the tree
Summer had come again for you and for me
Pink and white in the morning sun
A lovely day for children a new day had begun
A flock of birds took to the wing
Sailing around such joy did they bring
Looking up at the big, fluffy clouds
The children are playing and singing aloud
The cold, cold winter now in the past
Replaced by the summer, long may it last
The warmth of the sun beams down on the Earth
The tiny lambs leaping at spring's new birth
The dolphins are jumping out in the bay
And just like the children, have come out to play
The shadows now cover the end of the day
A light now shines from the Milky Way
Goodnight to the flowers, goodnight to you
Till tomorrow when all our dreams come true.

Charlotte Spawton (10)
Kingsham County Primary School

Big Ben

Big Ben
Strikes every quarter of an hour,
Tall, giant and loud!
Like a space shuttle,
Like a block of flats,
I feel tiny,
Like a particle inside a glass,
Big Ben,
Without it would time stand still?

Laura Chamberlain (10)
Kingsham County Primary School

It Can't Be, Can It!

A werewolf floats through the vampire doom
Of your bewildered hall and living room
But who can tell what he's trying to find
Sobbing with the sound of rushing wind
It can't be a poltergeist surely, you say to yourself
Peering over the thick glass sill
But the world out there is motionless and still.

As the werewolf flits across out there
The gloom filters through your part closed door
Blocking your mind with doubt once more
It's not a poltergeist, you say to yourself
Going out there to turn out the light
But the passageway is as pitch as night.

Jack Gatford (10)
Kingsham County Primary School

Mr Messy

Mr Messy,
Is so scruffy when you meet him.
He is an untidy, disgraceful, stupid little creature.
Always up to mischief,
Like a little troll.
It makes me feel superior,
Like Little Miss Perfect.
Mr Messy,
He is like a little prisoner which has been let free.

Chloe Ellis (10)
Kingsham County Primary School

It Isn't A Ghost, Is It?

A shadow glides into the midst of the silent darkness
Of your deserted corridor and lounge.
Nobody knows what he's attempting to discover
Screaming with the howling wind
'It isn't a ghoul,' you say to your mind
Peering through the casement clear
Still the planet outside, no whisper to be heard.

As the spirit zooms by, behind your room
A phantom shimmer covers the gloom
And slithers through your jarring door
Filling your brain with nightmares once more
'It isn't a ghoul' you whisper to your restless mind
Going round, back to dim the light
But still, the hall is ghostly and black.

You sit in your bed, and into your room
A ghostly figure comes out of the gloom.
A bat, a frog, a witch's spell
And a shadow, but no one can tell
what they're discussing behind the bed,
'It's a ghoul!' you say in your head
And run downstairs, and out of your bed.

You run to your mum, but my mum said,
'Why are you up now and out of bed?'
And I expect that's what your mum would say
If you ran downstairs, each and every day
You try to explain there's a monster upstairs
'There's is a ghost!' you shout, but nobody cares!

Abigail Harris (9)
Kingsham County Primary School

THE WEATHER CATS

My cat is the fog
Whirling round my legs
Bushy and soft to the touch
My cat is the fog.

The street cat's the lightning
Raging all night
Flashing over dustbins
The street cat's the lightning.

Granny Ginger is the sun
Snoozing in the yard all day
Lazing by the fire
Granny Ginger is the sun.

My kitten is the summer breeze
Flouncing, pouncing, swirling around
Taking life excitedly
My kitten is the summer breeze.

Emily Dyble (10)
Kingsham County Primary School

THE MERMAID

There she sits
Golden hair blowing in the wind
The seals are at her side
The birds call her name
While otters play around,
Dolphins and porpoises leap nearby.

She sits on her lonely rock
Singing her sweet tune
He eyes as blue as the ocean
A fish's tail she has
As bluey-silver as moonlight.

A man sees her
His sword is in his hand
He tries to catch the beautiful mermaid
But she slips away
Into the depths of the sea
The mermaid is gone.

Caitlin Ellis (9)
Kingsham County Primary School

A Flowering Thought

As I sit here I stare
Into the wild wonderland
Of bright colours
I know something is growing
My fingers move gently
Over a blank page

The colours are growing
I see it now, it's spurting
Out of the ground
It stops a moment again
Now and now and now

The dreams are uncurling
A pink velvet curve
The calm wind blows them
Shining in the summer sun

As night overtakes
The dream is fulfilled
The petals are sleepy
The wind has gone
The page is printed.

Zoe Yeldham (10)
Kingsham County Primary School

Silver Christmas

Slowly, silently, now the moon,
Walks the night in her silver shoes,
This way, and that, she peers, and sees,
Silver fruit upon silver trees.

One by one the casements catch
Her beams beneath the silvery thatch,
Couched in his kennel, like a log,
With paws of silver sleeps the dog.

Of doves in a silver-feathered sleep,
From their shadowy coat the white breasts peep,
A Christmas mouse goes scampering by.

With silver claws and silver eye,
And motionless fish in the gleam,
By reads in a silver stream.

Tiffany Hunt (10)
Kingsham County Primary School

Winter

Fluffy flying snowballs,
Zipping through the sky.
From the strong, white powder,
Falling from way up high.
Ball by ball,
Snowmen being built.
A blanket of snow,
Covers the roof.
Children foraging deep down on the ground,
For all the soft snow scattered all around.

Hannah Hawdon (10)
Kingsham County Primary School

Shades Of Meaning

A poltergeist pours continually through the shadowy twilight,
Of your disconsolate doorway and dining room,
And who can tell what he's inquiring for.
Howling with the effect of blustering wind,
It can't be a revenant, you say to yourself -
But the universe outside is hushed and tranquil.

As the incubus glissades by outside your abandoned room,
A ghostly glimmering replenishes the obscurity,
And percolates through your half-sealed door,
Contenting your mind with cynicisms once more.
It cannot be an apparition, you mumble to yourself,
Going outside to turn out the phosphorescence -
But the corridor is black as the pupil in your eye.

Stuart Osborne (10)
Kingsham County Primary School

Dracula

Dracula's castle is dark and slimy,
Dracula's skin is green and grimy.
He bites your neck and then he slurps,
He drinks your blood and then he burps!
He sleeps in his coffin deep underground,
The walls are so thick you can't hear a sound.
We can't wait till some young lad
Kills each vampire good and bad
And then maybe we can get some sleep,
Not lie in the grave while our necks leak.

Adam Taylor (8)
Kingsham County Primary School

Paws On Paper

Her coat as black as coal
Sleek and soft as ever can be
Her eyes are melting brown and deep
Her ears silky as silk can be
Food at the dozen one hundred pounds or more
Away, away, away as she chomps some more.

Wagging tail thump, thump, thump
As we walk down the stairs in the morning!
Her bed as warm as a bed could be
She likes her sleep while she dreams, dreams, dreams.

Her black, wet nose as she likes you
Wet when she wants to play
Her ears prick up.

Her puppy blind when she's young
Her mother's milk fills her tum
Whilst her father is drinking his rum
So look after your dog wherever you go
But remember your dog has a mind of its own!

Tom Clarkson (10)
Kingsham County Primary School

Ghost

The ghost,
Appears at night,
Awakened by a moon so bright.

The ghost,
Haunts a house,
Moves silent as a mouse.

The ghost,
Its presence fades,
As dawn light shades.

The ghost,
Gone, gone, gone.

Amy Ring (10)
Kingsham County Primary School

WINDOW PANE

I look out my window and I feel wrenched,
I see the homeless human beings suffering at Christmas.
There, I see people they have light blue lips,
Waiting to freeze,
I feel guilty.
Why do they have to die?
When I never seem to even cry at Christmas.

I feel like I have been lambasted in the heat,
I know not how they manipulate,
My heart is passionless like ice.

Lips as blue as the daylight sky,
Freezing, freezing like the Atlantic ocean,
His legs rustle and rattle like dry old bones.

A lonesome knuckled figure,
Stands alone,
The sight outside my window
Is as cold as the sea.

My thoughts are as vast
As the sky I can see,
My pain is like losing my own grandfather.

Jacob Moir (9)
Kingsham County Primary School

WINDOWPANE

When I looked out of my window,
I saw a lonely lifeless child.
Suddenly the frail fragile boy spoke,
How I wish my mum would let me give him a present.
I said to myself, why does he wish upon a golden star?
The dream might come true,
But change the subject,
In another garden,
I saw someone playing in the silky snow,
Why doesn't that homeless child do it?
Because I would,
That poor homeless child.
I want him to have a happy peaceful life with us.
This will not be true,
This young child is alone with no mum or dad.
His life is like the sky with no stars.
This gives me pain deep down in my heart
And the pain may never go.

Robert Buckland (10)
Kingsham County Primary School

THE LADY OF SHALOT

The river sparkles in the light,
The wolf howls into the night,
The Lady of Shalot had had a fright,
A mirror was sat in front of her so she might,
Look to Camelot.
But if she was to look out to the night or day,
She would not have a chance to stay,
If only the curse would go away.
She waited for her love to come and say,
'I will take you out of Camelot.'

There she stays throughout the year,
Watching people from far and near,
As silent and gentle as the deer.
A curse is on her, in which she must fear,
To look upon loved Camelot.
She weaves until the candle dies,
There she weeps and there she cries.
Then she sits and with a sigh,
'Oh how I wish that time would fly,'
Said the Lady of Shalot.

Natasha Cox & Cally Garfield (9)
Kingsham County Primary School

I SEE

I see the birds flying to the south,
Flapping their wings so gracefully,
Small birds, big birds, all of them are flying,
I see the birds flying to the south.

I see the lions prowling through the plains,
Lionesses hunting while the lions have a doze,
Small lions, big lions, all of them are sleeping,
I see the lions prowling through the plains.

I see the fish swimming in the river,
Swishing their tails silently,
Small fish, big fish, all of them are swimming,
I see the fish swimming in the river.

I see the plants sprouting their leaves,
Waving in the fresh summer's breeze,
Small plants, big plants, all of them are growing,
I see the plants sprouting their leaves.

Hayley Charlotte Creed (11)
Kingsham County Primary School

WINDOWPANE

I look out of my window
It was snowing,
Then I heard someone crying,
She should be buying
A tree, turkey, presents, and decorations,
I can see the pain in her eyes,
That pain I can feel inside.

But we can still sing and be happy with our families,
They make a fire to keep warm
And we have to stay till dawn.

25th of December Jesus Christ was born,
And they celebrate
Except the poor,
I feel angry, sad and ready to cry.

Chris Pearce (10)
Kingsham County Primary School

THE GREAT ESCAPE

In his chrysalis he sat
Soon to be a butterfly
Down did swoop the big blackbird
Here may be some lunch, he'd heard.

A tasty morsel he did see
He thought he'd have a grub for tea
A snap, a crunch, this could be lunch
But little did he know.

The biggest butterfly in town
Was just about to grow.
With a flap and a slap
The blackbird fell back
As the butterfly flew free.

Max Woods (11)
Kingsham County Primary School

THE WHITE SHADOW

The ghost in my house,
Lingers round.
In and out the living room,
The phantom creature shrieks and howls.
Sounding like raging thunder,
Drifting over to my back.
Flying over to me rapidly,
A cold, bitter breeze was about me!
Was it a ghost or was it my imagination?

I opened my mouth to scream,
But nothing came out.
I concentrated on this thing,
The thing came quicker,
Quicker than that!
Faster than you can dream of!

I looked at it feeling hopeless,
Not knowing what to do!
I panicked even more.
Suddenly it came right next to me,
Then suddenly it vanished!

Kayleigh Pope (9)
Kingsham County Primary School

My Blank Page

An unexciting, blank page,
A fragile, lifeless thing,
Like the whitest rose spread into a rectangular shape,
Like a shell with no smell.

The paper a line of pearls so white,
And the pencil makes it so grey and smudged,
This flat, crushed, white thing,
Like a field of white flowers.

A stale, blank page,
The paper wants an avalanche of words,
Like a bud that opens its petals to find a treasure within,
The paper glows like an open treasure box.

A stream of black ink kills its glowing ,white page,
And the page keeps its words like an oyster keeps its pearl,
The page is like a razor with words that scrape and stab,
And as I think about the blank page, I think about how beautiful it is.

Electra Ruddock (10)
Kingsham County Primary School

It Can't Be - Can It?

A shadow slides through the eerie night.
Of your abandoned conservatory and chamber
And who can explain what he is attempting to catch,
Howling with the echo of scurrying wind,
It cannot be a shadow, you whisper to yourself.
Glancing over the dusty casement,
But the night outside is noiseless and peaceful.

As the shadow glides beyond your utility room,
A spooky, glamorous gleam inflates the twilight
And strays through your private door,
Stuffing your thoughts with hesitation once more.
It can't be a shadow, you murmer in your mind,
Tiptoeing past to switch off the light.
But the corridor is as deadly dark as a prison cell.

Siân Agostinelli (10) & Natasha Cox (9)
Kingsham County Primary School

My Blank Page

My blank page
is as white as a fresh snowdrop.

That's my blank page
Looking at me
As I'm thinking how hard could it be?

Is it a page full of adventure or fantasy?

What shall you be,
My blank page?

My blank page,
What shall you be?

A map of the seven seas.

After lots of work that's what you'll be
Eventually.

Amanda Turner (11)
Kingsham County Primary School

WINDOWPANE

On a cold, chilling Christmas Eve,
I sit with my friend,
Talking about the hundreds of homeless people,
'We could turn out to be homeless,' I state!

'What makes you so sure?'
'What makes you so sure?'
I looked away, then looked back,
'Where did you go?'
It was then I realised she was tired
Of hearing of people homeless.

I looked out of the window
There she was freezing with her lips,
Pale as a blue broody sea,
'Come in at once, you have money!'
She just looked away.
She could no longer see.

I could see her black back from leaning against the pavement,
Her sour face and red nose began to disappear,
Her lost ears were red and wrinkled.
Tomorrow will be Christmas!
And she would no longer be here.

Lauren Huskisson (9)
Kingsham County Primary School

MY BLANK PAGE

My blank page,
Brimming with everything
I think as I glare into this wondrous bowl of possibilities.

My blank page,
It could be anything
As I look at my blank page I see a world of images.

My blank page,
What shall I do?
It sits there staring,
Urging,
Taunting me to utter the words of the world.

Karim Bedda (11)
Kingsham County Primary School

THE DAY . . .

The day has come for me, and a friend,
To go to a wonderful, exciting place, in Winchester,
A place of pure delight, of which I have only dreamed,
Marwell Zoo, a place where my sights will come alive.

We are going by car, a hot and sticky journey it will be,
It will roughly take thirty to forty minutes to get there,
I cannot wait to go to such a place,
A place where my sights will come alive.

We are just getting in the car, to get there,
The time is ten to nine,
so we will get there at twenty past ten or half past ten,
I am off to a place where my sights will come alive.

The view is outstanding, the countryside makes me glow,
All you can see is green, green and more green,
With a patch of yellow here and there,
A place where my sights will come alive.

Finally we got there, after forty miles,
My legs were numb,
We got to the ticket, but to find
It was not open today,
A place where my sights will not come alive.

Jake Stubbs (10)
Kingsham County Primary School

Thesaurus

To write something wise
With words old and
Second-hand,
Scooping your imagination
From off these pages
Hammering
Melting
The words together until
They fit
In glowing harmony,
And you have made your sentence.

But this is just the beginning,
And now we pull up our cuffs
And take a breath before
We start again.
Sawing,
Hammering
The pieces together until
They fit,
And you have made your small and second sentence.

Now you are getting started
To make a sentence
Full of words to fill
Your imagination
And so again
Melting
Hammering
Chiselling,
Until they fit again
And you are getting closer to
A small paragraph.
Closer to that small four lined
Paragraph.

Paragraphs so full of words and meanings
To build up pictures in your head,
Scooping words from these pages
Using words old and second-hand.
Hammering
Melting
Sawing
Chiselling
Until they fit
And leave it
All
Unperplexed and still.

Now you have made your paragraph.

Mathew Creed (11)
Kingsham County Primary School

MY BLANK PAGE

My blank page
Full of nothingness
How exciting
What to write

My blank page
I could draw a sea
How exciting
What to draw

My blank page
I could draw a waterfall
How exciting
What to think.

My blank page.

Matthew Dean (10)
Kingsham County Primary School

One Day I Woke Up In My Bed

One day I woke up in my bed
With funny things going round in my head
A princess sitting in a dragon's ear
A moose drinking a pint of beer
Walking fish on the sand
Elephants playing in a band
An apple flying with one wing
I didn't know that horses could sing
Dogs gliding in the sky
Hippos running madly by
Stars swooping carefully to me
A jumping, excited bumblebee
A dog itching out all its fleas
A bear holding some metal keys
One day I woke up in my bed
With funny things going round in my head.

Faith Farrow (9)
Langley Green Middle School

Night And Day

In the moonlight so, so bright
Up very high in the midnight sky
I can see a flashing light that shines
And shines throughout the night.

The dawn arrives and everything's light
And the birds are twittering with delight
People are waking for the day ahead,
Busy or not get out of bed!

Carly Stevenson (10)
Langley Green Middle School

HORSE RACING

I am a horse and I'm running a race,
My owner doesn't like it if I go my own pace
The jumps are high but the ground is low
I run like the wind when the man says *'Go!'*
The whip is stinging so I pick up speed
It's as if I'm a dog being strangled by a lead
I start to feel dizzy, I forget where I am
There's a field on my left and I can see a lamb
I was going along and my rider fell off
I didn't even realise until he gave a cough.
I can see the finish line, I hear a cry
I have to go back so I give a sigh
He jumps back on and says 'The trophy's mine!'
As we finally cross the finish line
My rider got a trophy and me, a rosette,
My rider's mum got some money because she won a bet.

Sarah Manners (11)
Langley Green Middle School

MY BEST FRIEND

I have a best friend but she lives in the scintillating ocean,
And helps me make enchanting potions.
She can dive and jump like an enormous whale
And has the exact same tail.
She can balance balls on her nose like a seal,
You wouldn't think my friend was real.
She's got flapping flippers and a fin
And has got grey-coloured smooth skin.

Samina Idris (11)
Langley Green Middle School

Crazy Zoo

Come on down to the crazy zoo,
The elephants jumped and the hippos flew,
The penguins flapped and the pigs mooed,
Welcome to the crazy zoo!

Come on down to the crazy zoo,
The zebras laughed and the lamas chewed,
The cats got drunk and the dogs wear tutus,
Welcome to the crazy zoo!

Come on down to the crazy zoo,
Jumping, laughing, flapping, mooing,
Flying, chewing and drinking;
This certainly is a crazy zoo!

Oliver Silviotti (11)
Langley Green Middle School

Henry VIII

King Henry was a roar,
He was as fat as a boar.
He had six wives,
But still wanted several more.
Jane Seymour,
He appreciated more,
But Catharine Parr
Lived far.

Krishna Patel (10)
Langley Green Middle School

Friendship Forever

Friendship is a blessing.
Without it, something in your life would be missing.
For all the special times we share.
For all the ways you show you care.
Sometimes we have fights and break up but then we make up.
Since the time we met, we've had to forgive and forget.
Think of all the fun times we've had,
We were always there for each other if we were sad.
Our friendship will last forever because we will always be together.

Misha Jechand (11)
Langley Green Middle School

Racism

I am black, you are white
There is no difference between you and me
Why do you make fun of me?
We are all the same

Why do you call me names?
Is it because of the colour of my skin?
It doesn't matter what you say
It doesn't hurt me in any way

Why don't you listen to what I have got to say?
You can hit me, you can scream
But I don't care because I love my race
And I am proud of my coloured face.

Saleem Ali (8)
Langley Green Middle School

A Starry Night

A starry night,
Beauty and fairness of the world
It gives me a bright light,
Millions and billions of stars come out tonight.

Give me knowledge and pride,
I dream I go to the sky and have a ride
Wish I could see a shooting star and slide,
Dreams are dreams, they're never going to glide.

People say stars are people,
But I believe that they are only the shining light
One day you might never know,
Stars might come alive.

Gayatri Patel (11)
Langley Green Middle School

Colours Of Harvest

Red is the colour of a juicy crunchy apple.
Yellow is the colour of sour sweet lemon.
Brown is the colour of a muddy fresh potato.
Orange is the colour of a cracking crunchy carrot.
Gold is the colour of a bunch of straight wheat.
Purple is the colour of a bright soft plum.
Green is the colour of a great big grape.
Blue is the colour of the fresh shiny sea.
White is the colour of white clouds.
Red, yellow, brown, orange, gold,
Purple, green, blue, white
Are all harvest colours!

Sandeep Nayee (11)
Langley Green Middle School

Dolphins

They're lovely, huggable and cute.
They will surely entertain you,
By doing somersaults and balancing balls on their nose.
Their cheeks are ruby red, they also like to pose.
If you ever had a chance with them they may be your new best friend.
They will mend your feelings in a sec,
By letting you have a go on them.
Flapping their flippers about while swimming underwater,
They're so unique.
I love dolphins, they're the best!

Sabrina Javed (11)
Langley Green Middle School

The Wondering Wicked Witch

Today I'll boil rats,
And then I'll feed my cats.
Today I'll make a spell,
Which I wish will work well.
When I was trying to catch a frog,
I suddenly tripped over a log.
Someone was knocking on the door,
When I opened the door I was amazed
It was crawling on the floor.
Today my friend brought two frocks,
But with holes in the purple socks.
Today I'll make a stew
Tomorrow I'll use you!

Kejal Mehta (11)
Langley Green Middle School

Pussy Cats

I love little pussy cats they're lovely and cute,
They're so adorable with their little funny boots.
They're friendly and kind with their astonishing caring hearts,
Be gentle with them like delicate blueberry tarts.
They're pretty and soft like beautiful butterflies,
Swaying around in the glistening, gleaming grass.
They jump and play as they do all day purring loudly as they pass.
Oh pussy cat, oh pussy cat you're so precious to me,
I am so pleased you're mine as you will always be!

Razia Rana (11)
Langley Green Middle School

Moon

Tonight the moon is very bright
Outshines the stars glittering light
What mystery this planet shares
With Earth its neighbour for many a year
Way back in time the two have seen
Miracles that only we can dream.

Katy Maxwell (11)
Langley Green Middle School

Space Race

There was an old man from space,
Who ran in a one mile race.
He said he would win,
But ended up in a bin
And returned to his home planet at pace.

Mousam Parekh (11)
Langley Green Middle School

A Strange Man

A strange man called today put every colour in a black sack
And took them away.

The tongue-tingling red of the strawberry ice lolly,
The twirly whirly turquoise of the wavy ocean,
The dark juicy blue of the squashed berry,
The lovely gold of the shiny smooth engagement ring,
The strange man put every colour in a black sack
And took them away.

Vidisha Nayee (11)
Langley Green Middle School

I Went Into Space

I went into space last night,
It was really cool
With aliens and cinemas and a swimming pool.
My mother said I was bonkers
But if she really knew,
She would say, 'What a night,' and would sigh 'phew.'

Ravi Parekh (9)
Langley Green Middle School

Horses

I love horses and ponies too,
I like to ride them out with you.
When it comes to the end of the day
I give him a big stack of hay.
I clean out his stable and make it all clean
So when he goes to sleep he has a sweet dream.

Sophie Ripley (10)
Langley Green Middle School

SNAKES

Long snakes, short snakes
Strong snakes, weak snakes
Outgoing snakes, shy snakes
Slimy snakes, dry snakes
Fat snakes, skinny snakes
Hissing snakes, quiet snakes
Fast snakes, slow snakes
Healthy snakes, ill snakes
Wild snakes, pet snakes.

Daniel Muggeridge (10)
Langley Green Middle School

GLORY, GLORY

Glory, glory,
Man U glory,
The champions of the world
Will reign forever be,
Till they lose a match
Which will never be,
So all the followers come together
And chant with me,
Glory, glory,
Man U glory.

Sagar Bakhai (9)
Langley Green Middle School

DREAMS

Dreams are like magic,
Trapped inside your head,
And they only get released
When you're all tucked up in bed.

Some dreams are happy,
Some dreams you cannot see,
But you should never fear a dream,
Because it's only what *you* make it out to be.

Rebecca Wall (11)
Langley Green Middle School

Hey Little Monkey

Through the jungle the monkey swings,
On the branches he hangs and sings.
He climbs on trees,
Seeing lots of bees.
He's never walking,
But always talking.
He doesn't live in a house,
He's so cute,
Hey little monkey give me back my boot!

Rabiah Mahmood (9)
Langley Green Middle School

I Know A Mum . . .

I know a mum who had a fat bum
She had a thumb as big as a plum
She put hats on her cats,
And when she said, 'Ha ha,'
She got hit by a car
And when she said 'Boo, boo'
She added '*I'll get you!*'

Ben Logan (9)
Langley Green Middle School

Dolphins

Dolphins have silky skin,
Shows to perform,
Hoops to jump through.
Dolphins love water.

Dolphins have songs to sing,
Babies to feed,
A mate to find.
Dolphins love water.

Dolphins have balls to play with,
Nose ball to play.
Dolphins really love the water.

Katie Everett (8)
Langley Green Middle School

My Monster Has . . .

Eyes as bright as the sun,
Mouth as miserable as a snake,
Head as smooth as a rugby ball,
Belly as scary as a face,
Fingers as small as some peanuts,
Legs as dark as a spider,
Nose as curvy as a pole,
Bones like marbles,
He is smaller than my leg.

Jamaine Khan (8)
Langley Green Middle School

WHO DID IT?

It was not me
Who broke the cup
And smashed the glass
And messed it up
It was my friend the alien
Not me!

It was not me
Who scared the dog
That chased the cat
Who broke the fence
It was my friend the alien
Not me!

It was not me
Who drew on the walls
And spilt the drink
All over the floors
It was my friend the alien
Not me!

It was not me
Who tore the book
And ripped the page
Saw the present and had a look
It was my friend the alien
Not me!

Emily Tester (10)
Langley Green Middle School

James The Teenager

I have this funny brother,
He acts like he's thirteen.
He gets all cross and moody,
And sometimes gets quite mean.

Now he thinks that girls are great,
But I think they're just a pain,
but when I get to his age,
I'll probably feel the same.

Michael Roberts (9)
Langley Green Middle School

Hidden Treasures

G one hunting treasure
O n a pirate ship
L anded on an island
D ig, dig, dig, dig, dig!

C ounted out ten paces
O ne to the left - six to the right
I n and out of bushes to find the right site
N othing will make us turn back
S omewhere around here is the right spot!

F ound the spot marked 'X'
O n a little hump
U nderneath some trees
N ear a smelly swamp
D iamonds is what we found
Time to all go home.

Rebecca Exall (9)
Lavant CE Primary School

Hidden Treasure

Hidden treasure, where? Where? Where?
Up here, down there,
I don't know where.
Six steps forward, six steps left,
'Come here quick crew, come and help!
I think I might have found it!
Oh look how much mess we have made!
Agh! But wait does the map say
Six steps forward or six steps back?
Oh it's OK it's six steps forward
Not six steps back!
OK carry on!
Oh look right there
Is it?
It is!
It's the hidden treasure
Ahoy my maties, ahoy for two!'

Megan Cowell (9)
Lavant CE Primary School

Hidden Treasures

T ogether we head towards the island
R eady to land this ship of ours
E astward bound
A ye, aye my captain
S harks are getting snappy
U nder the thundery sky
R acing through the puffs of wind
E ager to get the treasure
S eekers are getting near.

Laura Humphrey (8)
Lavant CE Primary School

HIDDEN TREASURE

Sailing in my boat to find,
Gold and silver of every kind.
I have got to the island where the treasure might be found,
The island I am on is big and round.
I have found a treasure chest that is yellow and old,
I pick it up and take it to my boat because I am cold.

Kirsty Blanks (8)
Lavant CE Primary School

HIDDEN TREASURE

Hidden treasure on the moon,
Space pirates must go soon.
Gold and silver rings,
Lots of precious things.
Hidden treasure on the moon,
Space pirates!
Must go soon.

Christopher Power (9)
Lavant CE Primary School

HIDDEN TREASURE

Ahoy me maties give me a slap
If you can find the treasure
Using this treasure map . . .
But first you must find the key.
Go through Parrot Jungle to find a useful tool,
Take it with you don't be a fool.

When you come out you'll find
The key to your chest
That includes a gold rupee.
Use the tool to cross Blood River,
If you fall in you get quite a shiver.
Finally go north west to find a treasure chest.

Jack Plant (9)
Lavant CE Primary School

Hidden Treasure

The pirates are coming
Hide the treasure
If you don't
They will take it with pleasure.

Katy McFarlane (8)
Lavant CE Primary School

Hidden Treasures

Hidden treasures, hidden treasures
I shall find you
Hidden treasures, hidden treasures
You're somewhere in the sand
Hidden treasures, hidden treasures
My flag by your spot
Hidden treasures
I've just hit the jackpot!

Freya Eggleston (8)
Lavant CE Primary School

HIDDEN TREASURE

It was exciting going on a treasure hunt.
I remember picking up a spade and digging.
First of all I found a plank of wood,
Then a lid, then a treasure box.
It had a skull face for a lock.

My cousins were there.
Daddy was there.
Brother and sister were there.
Two aunties and an uncle were there.
We were all excited, but I think I was the most.

Daddy and Uncle Toby lifted the box out of the hole.
It was very heavy.
We opened it.
There was an emerald, a diamond, multicoloured sand,
A piece of silver, pearl necklaces, a hook gold earring,

Five rings, a sharp knife, a bottle of rum
And lots more.
Daddy and Toby washed the sand out,
Then they carried it back
To the car.

We drove the car to our nannie's big house
And put the treasure in the far corner,
To the left of her shed
And shut the door.
We never mentioned another word about it again.

Lily Rigby (8)
Lavant CE Primary School

HIDDEN TREASURE

In the sand
Or in the ground
There's lots of treasure
To be found.

On the map
There is a cross
Soon the pirates
Will be lost.

When the treasure
Has been found
A hole is left
In the ground.

Thomas Cowell (7)
Lavant CE Primary School

THE GALES

Put your coats on,
Do your zip,
Pull on your gloves,
Stormy weather's coming.

Dark clouds crashing,
Trees are waving,
Tiles take-off,
Stormy weather's coming.

Walls waving,
Buildings shaking,
People shouting,
The stormy weather is here.

Oscar Behrens (8)
St Wilfrid's RC Primary School, Burgess Hill

SILVER

Hovering in the inky-black sky,
Drifting in a veil of stars,
Gliding down to a rather large house,
Touching it with a silvery hand.

How soft and gentle her moonlight glow
Rests upon the moonlit snow,
Dancing round the flower bed,
Turning roses to silver-red.

She looks upon the rolling hills
And finds a little child's window glistening in the dark.
Seeing the child asleep,
She scampers into the silvery hall and down the silvery stairs,
Then she dashes to the garden door
And gallops on the grass and jumps up to the stars.

Anjali Ramanan (8)
St Wilfrid's RC Primary School, Burgess Hill

SILVER

Hovering in the darkness of space, the moon wakes the air,
Floating over a galaxy of stars.
Slowly, silently she drifts through the sky,
Creeping over the inky-black night.
Calmly and gently she glides straight towards my silver home.
Peeping through my window she stared at me while I was sleeping.
Beaming onto the roof of our house,
She lit up a coat of silver.
Turning round, she started to turn the whole garden silver.
The grass turned as silver as a needle.

Harry Edwin Cooper (9)
St Wilfrid's RC Primary School, Burgess Hill

Moon

Hovering gently in the sky, shining brightly,
Creeping through breezy air,
Sweeping down to a smoking chimney,
Staring down at a silver table,
Starts to slowly glide down,
Turning silver the roof and chimney,
Lurking over a garden table,
Made that glowing silver,
Gently sailing over flowers,
Peering at the garden fence,
Flying further down the garden,
Landing slowly by the field,
Fainting down behind the hills,
As the birds come flying past.

Dominique Bell (9)
St Wilfrid's RC Primary School, Burgess Hill

The Moon

Lurking over the silvery world,
The moon is dazzling with joy.
Sailing through the sky with her glistening glitter
And saying goodbye to an audience of stars
Creeps the dark night into action.
Calmly the moon drifts to the smoky chimney,
The silvery smoke fills the air with its smell.
Gliding to the window, she sees a girl sleeping.
The glossy, green grass twinkles from her silvery coat.

Laura Richardson (8)
St Wilfrid's RC Primary School, Burgess Hill

SILVER

Slowly, silently, now the moon
Walks the night in her silver shoon,
She will touch the child in her silvery dream,
Casting a shimmering whisper of magic.
When her silver touch will fade,
No one will know
Where she has been.
She turns away to the midnight sky
With a touch of silvery dust,
She will become the glitter queen.
Everyone will love her silver stone
In the great shining star,
Winter will fall on the grass
With a sparkling touch of glass.
The silver reeds will become a shimmering stream
Of light and shine around the gleam.

Emma Jones (9)
St Wilfrid's RC Primary School, Burgess Hill

A SILVER MOON

Slowly, silently, up comes the moon,
Floating gently like sailing a big lagoon.
Speeds around quickly, not at all weak,
Like playing a game of hide-and-seek.
She always flies around at night
And floats around like a kite.
The windows reply in a happy way
When the moon shines her rays.
Then up comes the sun with the light led,
Now the moon has gone to bed.

Liam Davey (9)
St Wilfrid's RC Primary School, Burgess Hill

SILVER

Hovering in the darkness of space,
The moon gave life to the inky-black sky.
Dazzling over an audience of stars,
Sailing down, the dark night flies into action.
Creeping around the quiet house,
She touches the roof with a silvery hand,
Lighting up the roof a silvery-red.
Drifting down to the stream,
Swirling in silver the movement carries on,
Walking its way, like a child's song,
As he walks the grass to the roses.
Turning silver in a shining beam,
Touching rusty cars and windows,
Turn silver like glowing sticks.
People peering down the silvery dustbins,
Playing about with the last tins,
Gently gliding into the shed,
Calmly lurking about, turning shadows to silver.

Jamie Mitchell (9)
St Wilfrid's RC Primary School, Burgess Hill

THE MOON

Hovering in the darkness
Dazzling over the school of stars,
Flying high above the world,
Beaming its rays from space to Earth,
Dancing on my bedroom roof,
Sweeping back up to space,
Leaving millions of silver sparks,
Now the moon is spinning in space,
Glistening out all her silver.

Jordan Martin (9)
St Wilfrid's RC Primary School, Burgess Hill

SILVER

The shimmering moon calmly hovers
Around the sky.
In and out of the twinkling stars,
Slowly, silently spots a silver house
She wants to visit.
She magically puts her fingertips on
Everything she passes by.
Everything turns silver and
She gets to the house.
Slowly swaying, the trees are moving,
Sees the chimney blowing with silver smoke.
Calmly she passes the silver window,
She goes into the garden and
Makes the garden as beautiful as ever.

Bianca Kelly-Marques (9)
St Wilfrid's RC Primary School, Burgess Hill

SILVER

Slowly, silently now the moon
Walks the night in her silver shoon.
She hovers over the garden table,
Carefully flying, very able,
Passing twinkling stars as she goes,
Walking very softly on her tiptoes.
She looked upon the garden grass,
Turning it silver as she passed.
She heard something move, but only the fence,
Suddenly the grass moved up on the bench.

Charlotte Newell (8)
St Wilfrid's RC Primary School, Burgess Hill

Moon

Hovering over the Earth, the moon gave life to the sky,
Dazzling over an army of stars,
Beaming her silvery shine to the Earth.
She calmly starts to sail down.
Lurking round the street to spread her silvery pattern,
Flying to the house of stars,
She brightly shines silver all over the house,
Quickly running past the silvery windows.
Silently flying to the garden table with her see-through wings,
Slowly spreading silver with her silver hand,
Firmly dancing around the silver greenhouse,
Gently playing with the silver football on silver grass,
Creeping past the silver bedroom.
Upon the silver-coloured roof, she turns it rectangular.
The gentle silver roof appears.
Loudly staring through the window, she makes me silvery-green,
She gets her silvery dust out to solve the broken walls.

Charlie Howes (9)
St Wilfrid's RC Primary School, Burgess Hill

Silver

Slowly, silently now the moon
Walks the night in her silver shoon.
She rolls down to a garden and
Turns a flower frosty, silvery pink.
Creeping through the silver, dusty wind into my room,
She touches my quilt and it turns silvery-blue.
Calmly, the moon goes back outside
And it starts to rain with silvery water.
Slowly, the moon goes back
Up into the frosted, silver air.

Naomi Rocco (8)
St Wilfrid's RC Primary School, Burgess Hill

SILVER

Hovering in the darkness of space,
The moon gave life to the inky-black sky.
Dazzling over a school of stars,
Beaming at the darkness below.
Sailing calmly through space,
Glistening a silver light all around the world.
Calmly sailing down, down, down,
Gently touching the edge of the bed,
Turning it a beautiful silvery-red.
Touching it with a silver hand,
Turns around with the best ever grace,
Out of the window and up into space,
Brightly shining away again.

Rebecca McGowan (8)
St Wilfrid's RC Primary School, Burgess Hill

THE MOON

Slowly floating in the mist,
Calmly dazzling moon.
Silently land on the table,
Beaming the table with silvery dust,
Brightly but quickly touched my eye,
Creeping over the army of stars.
Sweeping down before my eye,
Gently swooping on the grass,
Making it silvery-green,
Shining on my bed,
Making it go silvery-red.

Daniel Cummins (9)
St Wilfrid's RC Primary School, Burgess Hill

Silver

Slowly in its cloud of mist,
A silent, silvery moment of bliss.
The silvery wind blows it away,
With a silver touch of thundery May.
Silently she whispers among silver trees
With fields of honey filled with glee!
She turns away and looks far back
To a silver-painted, tiny sack.
The silver fruit on the silver tree
Floats away in the silver sea.
Winter has nearly almost come,
Finding itself in silver fun.
She looks beneath a small stable,
Suddenly it turns into an enormous table.
She sees a bike and cures its rust,
With a tiny handful of silver dust.

Rachel Redmond (9)
St Wilfrid's RC Primary School, Burgess Hill

Silver

Slowly, silently, now the moon
Walks her night in her silver shoon
She quickly walks to the silver roses
When behind her the silver door quietly closes
Behind the shed there's a light of beam
Which makes her feel like she's in a dream
She flies around in her silver kite
So she can see the lovely silver sight
She walks down the garden to the shed
But all she could see was the colour silvery-red.

Sam Leighton (8)
St Wilfrid's RC Primary School, Burgess Hill

Power Wind Blowing

Put your coat on,
Buckle up the zip,
Pull on your gloves,
Wind racing through the street.

Grey clouds thundering,
Trees flying through the air,
People screaming and shouting,
Wind racing through the street.

Rivers overflowing,
People drowning,
Houses collapsing,
Wind ripping through the street!

Kancana Perez Ariakutti (9)
St Wilfrid's RC Primary School, Burgess Hill

The Moment Is Coming

Put your coat on,
Do up the zip,
Pull on your gloves,
The moment is coming.

Dark clouds floating,
Trees are blowing,
Brick walls rocking,
The moment is coming.

Big storms ahead,
Rain and wind,
Looks powerful,
The moment is here.

Matthew Muddell (8)
St Wilfrid's RC Primary School, Burgess Hill

Chasing Wind

Put your coats on,
Do up your zip,
Pull on your gloves,
Stormy weather is coming now.

Dark clouds coming,
Trees falling on homes,
The wind is calling,
Stormy weather is coming.

The storm is nearly here,
Tiles crashing to the ground,
Doors are rattling,
Windows are breaking.

Natalie Halsey (8)
St Wilfrid's RC Primary School, Burgess Hill

Whipping Wind

Put your coat on,
Do your zip up,
Pull on your gloves,
Stormy weather's coming.

Dark clouds thunder,
Rain falls fiercely,
Trees swing in the wind,
Stormy weather's coming.

Big trees flying,
Birds in the air,
Mud and grass fly,
Stormy weather's coming.

David Uden (9)
St Wilfrid's RC Primary School, Burgess Hill

Silver

Hovering in the darkness of space,
The silver moon lit up her array of stars,
Putting the blackboard away, bringing out the white one,
Sailing round the world, she wants to go to Ireland or France,
But she is coming to England.
Drifting and gliding down to Earth,
She says goodbye to her home.
She gets closer to my house with a little child.
Peering over my garden fence, looking for something to play with,
She touches my garden table and to her surprise, it goes silver.
She comes up a little to clean my room
And then says, 'I will be back, soon.'

Michael Thorn (9)
St Wilfrid's RC Primary School, Burgess Hill

Silver

Slowly, silently now she lurks,
Looking for something to shine on.
She lurks in every corner, looking for dark,
To conquer it with her silver warriors.
The garden table turns to silvery stone at the sight of her,
The greenhouse is now the silver house,
The shed turns from grey-brown to silver-grey,
She changes the world every night.
The life of the man on the moon lives every night,
The people of the world wait for her to come.
Her silvery coat covers the world with silver,
She's like a silver dove floating in the air,
Swiftly down, down, down, to put children to sleep.

Brendan Searle (8)
St Wilfrid's RC Primary School, Burgess Hill

The Moon

Gliding over the universe, shining like the sun,
Its silver rays control the sky while shooting through the night.
Swooping low, it touches a house roof,
Making it red and golden-brown.
Hundred upon hundred of stars watch with their glinting eyes.
Sparkling silver glows dazzle the horizon,
Shimmering gold rays shoot out from behind the seaweed-green hills,
Beaming, the moon flies behind them with the stars
And the glistening sun comes up.
Hovering in the sky, the sun brightens up the world.

Charlotte Heeney (9)
St Wilfrid's RC Primary School, Burgess Hill

Silver

Slowly, silently now the moon,
The silvery river turns into a lagoon.
Round the side, off she goes,
On her massive silver toes.
She runs with happiness and jumps with glee,
And runs around a silver tree.
She sneaks round to see the shed,
But instead bumps into my old bed.
Hovering, up comes the sun and
All her silver fun was done,
But when she faded away,
I knew she would be back another day.

George Martindale (9)
St Wilfrid's RC Primary School, Burgess Hill

SILVER

Slowly, silently now the moon
Walks the night in her silver shoon.
She looks to see the silver trees
And touches them with her silver breeze.

She sees a silver, gleaming stone
And stares at it, all alone.
A silver cat behind a silver car,
She looks at the world, near and far.

She looks down at the silver street
To find the cat she once did meet.
She looks down at the silver stream
And stares at the starlight gleam.

The silver birds in their silver nest,
Dying to meet their silver guest.
She looks and smiles at the birds,
They tweet and sing with tweeting words.

And then she starts to weep and cry,
All alone in the sky.
She will love a forever friend
And she will wait until the end.

Sophie Hunt (8)
St Wilfrid's RC Primary School, Burgess Hill

LIGHT POEM

Sunlight is a blinding sight,
Lots of kids play with a kite.
The kites fly at an unbelievable height,
But when it starts to get dark, you may have a fright.

Michael McFadden (8)
St Wilfrid's RC Primary School, Burgess Hill

A Killing Wind

Put on your coat,
Do up your zip,
Pull on your hat,
Stormy weather's coming.

Dark clouds thunder,
Rain thrashing down,
Rooftops snapping,
Stormy weather's coming.

People running about,
Loud dogs barking,
Garden tables flying,
Stormy weather's coming.

Jessica Crowhurst (8)
St Wilfrid's RC Primary School, Burgess Hill

The Great Storm

Put on your coats,
Do up your zip,
Pull on your gloves,
Stormy weather's coming.

Dark clouds clump,
Ripped trees flying,
Roof tiles flying,
Stormy weather's coming.

Squeaking doors,
Rattling windows,
Cars crashing,
Stormy weather's coming.

Charlie Dykes (9)
St Wilfrid's RC Primary School, Burgess Hill

Moonlight Poem

M oonlight is bright.
O ur houses shine when the moon is shining
O ver the trees and flowers are shining because the moon is shining.
N ever go out when the moon is shining.
L ight is bright, everything is shining.
I t is nice when the moon is bright.
G oodnight moonlight.
H owever the moon is bright,
T ogether the moon and stars are bright.

Victoria Marshall (9)
St Wilfrid's RC Primary School, Burgess Hill

Horses Are The Best

Horses, horses, are the best,
I don't care for the rest.
Barny, Barny, is the best,
But I still like all the rest.
Riding, riding, here you are,
Now let's go really far.
Take them, take them, here you are,
Take them to the school so far.

Lesson, lesson, don't be late,
Come on through the gate.
Lunge lead, lunge lead, lead me round,
Take it off and turn around.
Gallop, gallop, canter, trot,
We all ride quite a lot.
Stable, stable, here we are,
I've never been so really far.

Chelsea Hennessey (7)
St Wilfrid's RC Primary School, Burgess Hill

WINDY WEATHER

Put your coat on,
Do up your zip,
Pull on your gloves,
Stormy weather's coming.

Dark clouds storming,
Rain going in all directions,
Garden tables flying,
Stormy weather's coming.

Don't go outside,
You might fall over.
It's very windy,
Stormy weather's coming.

Isla Pithie (8)
St Wilfrid's RC Primary School, Burgess Hill

WIND

Put on your coat,
Do up your zip,
Pull on your gloves,
Stormy weather is coming!

Dark clouds thunder,
Rain dashes sideways,
Water flowing fast,
Stormy weather is coming!

Tiles are blowing,
People are screaming,
Water flowing fast,
Stormy weather is coming, help!

Alex Adair (9)
St Wilfrid's RC Primary School, Burgess Hill

Bright Light

M ountains underneath the moonlight sparkling bright silver,
O ver all the cities and towns shines bright moonlight,
O utside Earth shines the big, bright moon,
N ever stops shining, so Earth has light at night,
L ight shines as bright as it can,
I t's not as bright as the sun, but it's bright enough,
G ives us light for the night so we can see,
H elps us see all around in the dark,
T ries to be as bright as the sun.

Michael Hamlet (8)
St Wilfrid's RC Primary School, Burgess Hill

The Magic Castle

Long ago in a town at night,
A moon shone so bright, oh bright.
Below a castle stands so tall,
Where witches hold great parties and balls.

Two children stood gazing up,
Watching the party begin to erupt.
They see the clock strike the witching hour
And then the clouds begin to shower.

The witches become evil and bad
And sometimes become a little mad.
In the morning it is very quiet,
The witches have gone, I am so *surprised!*

Hannah Bishop (8)
St Wilfrid's RC Primary School, Burgess Hill

Tearing Wind

Put your coat on,
Do up your zip,
Pull your gloves on,
Stormy weather thundering through the air.

Dark clouds crashing,
Rain is coming from a height,
Wind pulling up natural things,
Stormy weather thundering through the air.

Clouds gathering,
Clouds thundering,
Rain coming,
Stormy weather thundering.

India Pain (8)
St Wilfrid's RC Primary School, Burgess Hill

Lightning, Thunder

Put your coats on,
Button your coats,
Pull on your gloves,
Wind's ripping through.

Dark clouds thunder,
Trees falling down,
Rain is coming,
Wind's ripping through.

Floods rushing past,
Houses get soggy,
Cars get wet,
Wind's ripping through.

Marnix van Gelderen (8)
St Wilfrid's RC Primary School, Burgess Hill

They All Went Off Down The Road

They all went off down the road,
A frog, a newt and a toad.
They went to a shop
And saw a good top
And the frog jumped over the toad.

They all went off to the fair,
The fly, the bee and the bear,
They went on a carousel
And rung the bell,
So then they sat down in a chair.

They all went off to the zoo,
The bee and the kangaroo,
They looked in some cages
And read pages and pages
About animals and friends of theirs too.

They all went off to the house,
The cat, the dog and the mouse,
Then they said,
'It's time for bed!'
And then they went off somewhere else.

Georgina Logue (7)
St Wilfrid's RC Primary School, Burgess Hill

A Beaming Poem

Sunlight is light alright,
No need to light a light.
A slight light from the sunlight,
It's such an attractive sight.

William Boyce (9) & Phil Stetter (8)
St Wilfrid's RC Primary School, Burgess Hill

COLOURS

Red is some paper,
Red is your blood.
Yellow is a round banana,
Yellow is a hot fire.
Blue is the cold sea,
Blue is the flower, bluebell.
Green is the tall grass,
Green is a jumping frog.
Orange is a round orange,
Orange is the boiling sunset.
Pink is your flexible skin,
Pink is a fat pig.
Purple is lipstick,
Purple is a party dress.
Black is the scary dark,
Black is the sky at night.
Brown is your hair,
Brown is a paint.

Natasha Miller (8)
St Wilfrid's RC Primary School, Burgess Hill

THE SUNLIGHT

When I was a child I thought
The sun was a huge daffodil,
The sun was a huge sunflower.

The sun was a chunk of butter,
The sun was a chunk of cheese.
Now I see the sun is just a sun.

Abigail Stribbling (8)
St Wilfrid's RC Primary School, Burgess Hill

Cauldron Chant

Bubble, bubble,
Cauldron spin,
Bubble, bubble,
Swan's wing.
Trouble, trouble,
Witches, wizards,
Trouble, trouble,
Start a blizzard.

Bat's wing, cat's tail,
Monkeys' cling, dog's nail,
Sparrow's cheep, frog's leap,
Cheetah's run, elephant's tongue.

Bubble, bubble,
Snowdrop.
Bubble, bubble,
Horses clip-clop.
Bubble, bubble,
Toil and trouble.

Witches sprinkle, witches smile,
Without this all spells would fail.

Ellen Murtagh (8)
St Wilfrid's RC Primary School, Burgess Hill

Blazing Sun

When I look so high in the sky,
The sun looks like a yellow bowling ball.
It also likes like a red ball,
And when it's high it looks like dragon's fire.

Daniel Forman (8)
St Wilfrid's RC Primary School, Burgess Hill

At The Funfair

Ding-a-ling-a-ling!
What is that I hear?
I know,
The funfair must be near!
Round and round the merry-go-round,
Red and yellow and blue,
Blurs in my eyes as it zooms faster.

Later on, it's ice cream,
Followed by the dog race team.
I'm puffing out my chest with pride
As I'm whizzing down the slide.

I'm bouncing on the bouncy castle,
I bounce like a little rascal.
Now I am going home,
Away from all the beautiful colours.
Hang on . . . stop the car quick -
I'm going to be sick!

Maria Adlam (8)
St Wilfrid's RC Primary School, Burgess Hill

My Dog

I have a dog called Jack,
He's white with spots of black.
He loves his food
And he will always be in a happy mood.
He can do really clever tricks
And he never bites, he just licks.

Catherine Birnage (7)
St Wilfrid's RC Primary School, Burgess Hill

Red

Red can shine really bright,
Red is a wonderful sight.
Red is a bell,
Red makes a nice shell.

Red is a heart,
Red can break apart.
Red is a car,
Red can go far.

Red is a pencil pot,
Red is hot.
Red is a van,
Red is a frying pan.

Red is blood
Dripping from your hand.
Red is a light,
Red is a band.

Red is a spot,
Red is a dot,
Red is a pen,
Red is a hen.

Red can be good,
Red can be bad,
Red can be normal,
Red can be mad.

Frances Maltby (7)
St Wilfrid's RC Primary School, Burgess Hill

A Christmas Tree

A
Christmas tree
Is shiny. It glitters
In the window, a couple
More things, like a star and
Baubles, tinsel, lights, and of course,
Presents which I like best, but that's not
The true meaning of Christmas. It is that
Jesus will be born!

Joanna Lindsay (7)
St Wilfrid's RC Primary School, Burgess Hill

My Mum

A tree grows way up high in the sky
And my mum sings me a lullaby.
My mum stares at me and so do I,
She sings me to sleep and says goodbye.

Megan French (7)
St Wilfrid's RC Primary School, Burgess Hill

Pooh Bear

Shaggy, old, raggy bear,
Plays all day in the mud and never gets out.
He's Pooh Bear, that's who he is.
He eats shiny honey all day long.
I have to go now, so I will see you again,
Very soon.

Francesca Quilley-Smith (7)
St Wilfrid's RC Primary School, Burgess Hill

Spaghetti, Spaghetti

Spaghetti, spaghetti, my favourite thing,
I could eat it all up in only one minute.
Spaghetti, spaghetti, my favourite thing,
I just can't resist it whatever I do.
Spaghetti, spaghetti, my favourite thing,
Wherever I go I will think about it.
Spaghetti, spaghetti, my favourite thing,
Whenever I go to a restaurant I will order spaghetti.
Spaghetti, spaghetti, my favourite thing,
How could I live without it!
Spaghetti, spaghetti, the greatest thing!

Alice Cannon (7)
St Wilfrid's RC Primary School, Burgess Hill

Angels

Angels' wings are white as snow, all silky and smooth,
Their hair is golden like the bright sun which is so fine,
Their hearts are so nice and caring, but most of all, friendly.
Their bodies are smooth and clean,
Their lips are as red as roses that shimmer,
Their eyes are blue, they glitter like the wavy sea.
Their faces are so shiny, they look like stars.
Their clothing is nice and yellow,
It looks like fluffy cotton wool.
Their halo is glittery gold, it shines above them.

Jemma Hill (10)
Sidlesham Primary School

Birds

Birds, birds, fly around,
Never stop for a rest.
They fly around all
Day and night.

Some eat mice and
Some eat worms,
Some eat something
Different.

Birds that are grown,
Birds that are white,
Birds that are multicoloured.

Some have long beaks,
Some have short beaks,
Birds, birds, they're sweet
And colourful and sing
Out loud, oh, I love birds.

Chloe Coppin (10)
Sidlesham Primary School

Sweets

S weets, yummy for your tummy,
W hite sweets, red sweets, green sweets,
E at them at red-hot speed.
E veryone likes sweets,
T ime for the sweet shop to open.
S crumptious sweets.

Ben Parker (11)
Sidlesham Primary School

The Word Of Gold

Gold is shiny,
Gold is bright,
Whether it's 18 carat,
Whether it's white.

Gold in a ring,
In a necklace too,
Gold for me,
Gold for you.

Gold on cups,
Plates that shine,
Knives and forks,
Not on mine.

Jewellers' shops,
Argos too,
Gold for me,
Gold for you.

Gold to say,
'I love you,'
Gold to say,
'Yes, I do.'

Pirates' treasure
To be found,
Gold and diamonds
To astound.

Oh what beauty
For all to see,
Gold for you
And gold for me.

Kelly Watts (8)
Sidlesham Primary School

HIDDEN TREASURES

Hidden treasures in the sea,
One for you and one for me.
One for Mum, one for Dad,
One for every little lad.
Would you like to have one too?
You can get one at the zoo.
Lion, tiger, chimpanzee,
All can come to us for tea.
Hidden treasures in the sky,
Would you really like to try?
Would you like to see a star,
Shining near and shining far?
Hidden treasures in the sun,
To catch one would be fun.
Starfish crawling on the beach,
Can't catch it, it's out of reach.
Hidden treasures in the fire,
Could be caught up in barbed wire.
Pretty blue and yellow flame,
Try to touch them once again.
Hidden treasures in our home,
Heath and warmth, electric light,
Shining in the home so bright.
Hidden treasures in the car,
Can take us so near or far.
Take us round and round the street,
Lots of friends for us to meet.
Back to the treasures in the sea,
Now it's home, it's time for tea.

Michaela Collins (9)
Sidlesham Primary School

Fly Away Home

The mythical owl sits in his palace,
The palace of evergreen magic.
He strokes his long, dusty robes
And soft white diamond wings.

He looks at the black-dyed sky
And watches crystals set in
An unexplored patchwork quilt
Inside a midnight fantasy far away.

He turns his head and sighs,
He screeches a loud siren of cunning hunger.
Just as he flies past an old oak tree,
He hears a twig break.

His eyes start to glow.
Suddenly he swoops down,
He perches in a birch tree
And gulps his take-away down.

He had a little brown mouse,
So tiny against the powerful wizard-bird.
He is the king of nocturnal darkness,
He snuggles up nice and warm for the long trip
Back to where he belongs.

Over the bare, naked trees,
Over the glowing houses,
Over the frozen lakes,
He passes his friends.
He finds his home,
He curls up warm
And goes to sleep.

Charlotte Manley (10)
Sidlesham Primary School

WILDLIFE

Lions are so fluffy.
Lions are so frightening.
Elephants are as fat as a sumo wrestler.
Monkeys like to swing about in the trees.
Zebras have so many stripes.
Camels have the hump sometimes.
Crocodiles came for a snap.
Whales splashing in the water for you and me.
Sharks feeding on their food.
Armadillos running free.
Deer being as silent as they can.
Pigs as dirty as they are.
Cats purring just on me.
Dogs barking at my cat.
Chickens just clucking about.
Goats run at me.
Foxes sneaking up on a chicken,
Mice sneaking cake off me.
Hamsters taking seeds out of pots.
Bears eating my dad.
Rabbits running as fast as they can.
Birds flying as high as trees.
Ducks picking on William.
Horses clopping on the street.
Snakes hissing in a tree.
Lizards munching insects.
Tortoise swimming in the sea.
Anteaters eating ants.
Bees buzzing in the trees.
Owls hooting in the sky.

Max Anderson (10)
Sidlesham Primary School

A Roast Dinner

At Nanny's I get so excited,
Especially on a Sunday.

Do you know why?
Because of Sunday lunch!
Granny makes the best roast.

R oasted potatoes,
O rangey carrots,
A ccompanied by leafy broccoli,
S tuffed chicken,
T horoughly coated in gravy.

At Nanny's I get so excited,
Especially on a Sunday.

At first we have a little chat
About families and all that,
Then we got to the juicy bits,
The food, of course,
I lick my lips and tuck in!

The chicken is just as juicy,
The potatoes are just as crispy,
The carrots are just as tender,
It's all the same . . . except the gravy is even richer!

At Nanny's I get so excited,
Especially on a Sunday.

My tum is nearly full,
I can hardly eat!
I'm really sad
Because we have to go soon.

At Nanny's I get so excited
And now you know.

Sophie Levens (9)
Sidlesham Primary School

THE ELEMENTS

As I gaze into the wicked fire, I can almost
Feel the flickering flames licking my sides,
Like snakes they sway in the breeze
And light up the entire room with a warm glow.
I feel the heat wash over me like sinking into a hot bath.
When it dies, it's like the happiness fading from the empty grate.

I dive swiftly into the cool, clear water and swim deep,
Deep down to the very bottom.
In my mind, I see small tropical fishes flitting and darting
In-between the waving seaweed hidden treasures
Lay buried beneath the silky sands, but when I stop imagining,
All I see is the dirty bottom, littered with rocks.
I try to imagine it again, but it's like trying
To hold water in my hands, it seeps away.

When you see the world, it is a dark blue,
A mottled green, and a lot of swirling mist (clouds),
But look a little closer and you'll see towering blocks of civilisation
And seas stretching as far as the eye can see.
You'll see nasty things too, like gases wafting into the sky
And ships pouring oil into the sea, and it's spoilt.

Holly Pickering (11)
Sidlesham Primary School

Space

Spaced, beautiful and big,
With planets spinning around and around,
Floating in space without a sound.
Comets and stars and meteors too,
Neptune still green with a hint of blue.
The sun is shining in a blaze,
Astronomers still look at it in a gaze,
Maybe an eclipse will happen soon.
Is that man still up on the moon?
The solar system is quite cool,
Except for when you have to learn the planets at school.
I could go up and see Mars,
But I'll stay down here with my Mars bars!

Patrick Wingrove (11)
Sidlesham Primary School

Winter

Winter, winter, as white as snow,
Cold and dark, very dull, boring and sad,
Scarves and overcoat keep you warm.
One thing you need is hot cocoa and a cup of tea.
Winter is better outside in the snow, making snowmen
And rolling about in the snow.
But summer is the best time of the year,
Warm nights, really hot days and cool, long days,
Being allowed to wear shorts and t-shirts outside
In the warm sun and hot weather
With all my friends.

Jamie Corbett (10)
Sidlesham Primary School

Planet Tix

Burning bright it shines,
The gateway to another world,
Burning red, fiery orange, scarlet, yellow,
Spinning, swirling in the middle,
What a sight.
Stretching across the galaxy,
It pulls me down further and further,
Spinning, spinning, faster and faster,
Through I go,
Silent, silent, so scary silent.
Where am I?
Who are you?
Who am I?
'We are the people from inside this world,
The Tixilixies is our name.'
Their hands are green with purple spots,
Their heads are red,
Seven eyes,
Whatever next?
They hit me with a hurling hex,
I'm tied to a post.
Hang on, who are you?
'Me Chief Tixilixie.
You're our prisoner.'
Suddenly I felt a knife cut me free,
I ran and ran back to the ship.
Up we go,
Thrusters at maximum,
And away.
Goodbye Planet Tix.

William McGovern (11)
Sidlesham Primary School

WILDLIFE

Monkeys like to play about,
Elephants sit bathing in mud,
Hyenas laugh like babies,
Crocodiles swim in the swamps.
Lions feasting and feasting some more,
Shark eating fish,
Whales eating sharks,
Zebras galloping from cheetahs,
Armadillos running in the green.
Camels humping along,
Pigs oinking in the sty,
Cats purring on the wall,
Dogs chasing cats.
Cows pooing, what a *smell!*
Chickens, chickens, laying, laying,
Foxes spying in the day,
Foxes murdering in the night.
Hamsters eating day and night,
Rabbits munching on carrots,
Bears gobbling Gabriels,
Horses galloping on the lawn,
Ducks flapping about.
Geese, white and fluffy,
Birds swooping in the sky,
Snakes sliding in the sand,
Lizards munching on insects,
Tortoises swimming in the blue,
Anteaters eating ants,
Bees buzzing in the air,
Screech owls screeching and some more.

Harry Richardson (10)
Sidlesham Primary School

HIDDEN TREASURES

Up in the attic,
In the eaves,
Through the darkened cobwebs,
Over the dusty boxes,
To a loose floorboard.
Underneath is a
Tiny box with silver hinges,
Black and white photos,
In smart clothes,
A tiny locket.
Inside it says,
'Peace shall be forever
To thy owner.'
There is a bear
Which Mum says was her old one,
But it's lost lots of fur.
Then there is a diary,
Which we have read pages from.
Next, an ivory tusk from an elephant,
From when my parents went to India.
Something I found yesterday,
Hidden in a drawer in the box.
Inside was a scroll tied with ribbon.
Mum said it was the family tree.
I asked her did she know where other treasures were,
She said she stored them in her head.

Frances Bell (9)
Sidlesham Primary School

The Hummingbird

The amazing hummingbird's gentle, warming voice
Soothes across the canopy.
Its unique beak sucking the succulent pollen
As it hovers over the sweet-smelling flowers.
Her feathers so delicate and scarlet,
Her magical, dainty wings beating in the sun's rays,
She glides through the striking sunset,
Then nightfall comes as she snuggles up in her nest
And settles to sleep.

Frankie Beavis (10)
Sidlesham Primary School

Footie

F ootball is great,
O oooh, it makes me shout.
O h it hit the bar.
T wo minutes left.
I missed an open goal.
E very footballer has to have skill.

Lawrence Clifton (11)
Sidlesham Primary School

Sorry Miss

Sorry Miss, I was late,
I was eating my cake,
My car wouldn't start,
So I had to go in a cart.
Sorry Miss, my mind was elsewhere,
My thoughts were far away.

Liam Cattermole (10)
Sidlesham Primary School

Stargazing

Stars are giant suns
Floating in space,
A million miles away.
Some in groups,
Some in constellations,
Then the sun in the middle,
Which scientists study.
Millions of white pinpricks,
The stars are
Scattered across the sky.

Emma Smart (10)
Sidlesham Primary School

The Night Has Come

The night has come,
Yippee, yum, yum.
Sausages sizzling round,
All fat and stumpy,
Fireworks shooting up, up, up
Into the air.
Bang! Bang!
Yes, the night has come . . .
That's it . . . it's gone.

Hannah Gibson (8)
Southwater Junior School

Turtle

Gracefully swimming in the sea,
Oh, what a lovely place to be.

Andrew White (9)
Southwater Junior School

The Magic Box

I will put in the box;
A smelly spell on a snowy night,
A rolling rabbit in a rocking boat,
The screech of an eagle on an autumn day.

I will put in the box;
The buzz of a bee busy in the sun,
A tiny T-shirt of a tiny teddy,
The feeling of a foot treading on a piece of glass.

I will put in my box;
The feeling when somebody gently tickles you,
The first munch of a rosy red apple eaten on a spring morning,
The lick of a cold ice-lolly on a summer's morning.

I will put in the box;
The tired feeling after my first technology lesson,
The smell of my lovely dinner cooking,
The excited feeling of playing the recorder for the first time.

My box is velvet with golden hearts on the lid.
It has got caramel as the hinges and if you lick the box,
It will taste of toffee.
On the sides there are snowflakes and snowmen.
My box is very special to me.

Louisa Clark (8)
Southwater Junior School

The Magic Box

I will put in the box
The sparkling sand touching the tip of my toes,
The spiky shell, shaped as a star,
Ballet shoes as pink as a bright pink pig.

I will put in the box
A mermaid's necklace that's fallen from a cliff,
A slipper that sparkles and shimmers in the moonlight,
Then the last petal of a red rose.

Imogen Seear (8)
Southwater Junior School

The Magic Box

I will put in my box,
A precious piano playing beautiful music,
A magical rosy rabbit with rainbow-rich fur,
A beautiful bed that's bouncy, covered with beanies.

I will put in my box
A super star that shines and sparkles brightly in the sky,
A strange-shaped swimming pool where you lie and relax,
A scary, spooky sound of a ghost.

I will put in my box
The sound of a bad tiger *roar!*
My smiley family who always smile at me,
The taste of warm soup when you're ill,
A thirteenth month that turns everyone upside down.

I will put in my box
A turning turkey, turning around.

My box is made of gold and silver,
You have to find gold to open it.
It is decorated with moons and beautiful stars.

Charlotte Rodrigues (8)
Southwater Junior School

The Rattlesnake

He slithers across the soft sand
While his friends play the rattlesnake band.

He slithers across the road
While his friends are eating toad.

The rattlesnake is eating a leech,
While he's sitting on the beach.

While the chickens are going peck, peck, peck,
The rattlesnake thinks he's a nervous wreck.

He slithers across a person's neck,
Oops, that person is Gregory Peck!

Gregory McClarnon (9) & Anthony Duhig (8)
Southwater Junior School

Isabel Ventures Further

Isabel met an ugly, fat toad
As she was walking down the road.
The toad was warty, the toad was fat,
He could easily squash a full grown cat.
He said, 'Beep, beep, I'm in a fright!
I've only just got my meal for tonight!'
Isabel, Isabel didn't worry,
Isabel didn't scream or scurry.
Isabel looked at him very hard,
And squashed him flat with a nearby bollard.

Eleanor Robins (9)
Southwater Junior School

Dolphins

Dolphins do the most stunning flips,
They also give you affectionate nips.

They play with you in the sun,
I wish I could keep one but mind you, they weigh a ton.

They are lovely creatures,
They have stunning features.

They eat fish
For their dinner dish.

They swim in the deep, blue sea,
They can also swim with you and me.

Everyone thinks she is number one,
Apart from the fact that she can't run.

She splashes and splashes all day long,
At the end of the day, she sings her little song.

Abigail Whittaker (9)
Southwater Junior School

Snowman

I want to build a snowman,
I want to build him nice and tall.
I want to build a snowman,
To look above one and all.

I want to build a snowman,
To tuck me in at night.
I want to build a snowman,
Build him with all my might.

Amy Johnson (9)
Southwater Junior School

A Night To Remember

Fireworks go off late at night,
In the darkness, they glow like shimmering torches.
Traffic lights,
I love the way traffic lights go off,
Red, amber, green.
Sparklers,
I love the way you sparkle in the late night breeze.
Catherine wheel,
I love the way you turn and spin, round and round you go;
You are so beautiful.
Rocket,
I love the way you shoot into the sky and
How you explode into little bits.
The fun has ended for this year
And another 5th of November to remember.

Nicolas Heath (7)
Southwater Junior School

Moonlight

Watching all the cars
Surrounded by moonlit stars.

Below, outstanding flowers
That you could stare at for hours and hours.

The stars are so bright,
It's such a peaceful night.

The sun appears,
The birds' song catches your ears.

Ellen Powell (9)
Southwater Junior School

My Magic Box

I will put in my box
The rattling breath of a fearsome dragon,
An ancient map that shows you the way to another realm,
The happy dreams of a child.

I will put in my box
A gaunt ghost with glittering eyes,
The magic, straight from the fingers of a wizard
And a scarlet sky.

My box has a golden dragon engraved on the lid
And in the shadows, the galaxy is hiding.
My box is made out of the weather
And it will never break.

Drew Taylor (7)
Southwater Junior School

Adventures Of Isabel

Isabel met a tall, thin giraffe
As she was taking a boiling hot bath.
The giraffe had fangs as sharp as a pin
And when he roared, he made such a din.
The giraffe said, 'Hi, I'm pleased to meet you,
Now pass me my napkin and now I can eat you.'
Isabel, Isabel didn't worry,
Isabel didn't scream or scurry,
She put on a spell and made the giraffe shrink,
She then strolled to the door, but banged into the sink.

Gemma Schofield (9)
Southwater Junior School

INTERGALACTIC BATTLE

Fearless heartbeats, pumping hard,
My sword rattling by my side,
Sweat dripping down my face,
Looking around at the wide space.

Suddenly the ground begins to shake,
Enemy begins to awake.
Endless fear sweeping through,
It's funny how they look so fake.

Creeping slowly on the ground,
Praying that they won't turn around,
Hands trembling, reaching forth,
Clutching swords, heading north.

My mouth opens and shouts, 'Attack!'
The ground beneath me starts to crack.
Fellow army starts the battle,
While Martians turn at the double.

Now there is no turning back,
It's no use, I have to attack.
Suddenly a thought zips through my mind,
I don't want to attack, I want this to end.

Then I turn and see the blade
Glistening in the sun.
I hear a scream, perhaps my own,
My legs just will not run.

I always feared this moment would come.
A stab in my heart
And now I am gone.

Irene Messinger & Roberta Doggett (11)
Turners Hill CE Primary School

My Friend

Do not leave me,
Never deceive me,
Just believe in me,
Please, my friend.

Care and love me,
Kiss and hug me,
Just don't doubt me,
Please, my friend.

Hand losing, grip me,
Falling down a cliff from me,
Just don't let go thee,
Help me, my friend.

Loyalty running out from thee,
Faith is losing power from thee,
Heart beating quickly,
Goodbye my friend, lost forever.

Isabelle Leach (8)
Westbourne Primary School

The Way To God

A church stands forever,
Its yews with
Their imploring branches,
Swaying, shielding
From pouring rain,
Its everlasting path
Leading into Heaven,
House of God
Forever.

Eugenia Popesco (8)
Westbourne Primary School

THE GRAVEYARD POEM

Stones make me silent,
Can make me lonely.
There is sometimes ivy on gravestones,
They can be a pretty sight.
You can't read all the writing, it's so old.
Pictures on the church windows tell stories,
Tell stories of Jesus.
Sometimes there is a cross,
A cross with the Son on,
The Son, who died to save his people.
Stones make me silent.

Pamela Clark (8)
Westbourne Primary School

FOREST

As old as my grandad,
Like a vegetation battlefield.
Reaches the sun,
Let it live.

Like the biggest mountain,
As delicate as a rose,
A beast's refuge.
Let it live.

Like a crowded maze,
As dark as the back of your mind,
Life to all.
Let it live.

Anthony Davies (10)
Westbourne Primary School

Under The Yews

Six hundred years it has stood,
Stands again,
Tip of its reaching steeple,
Entices,
Pray, worship,
Always feels mysterious,
Watches weddings,
Makes you feel lonely.

Hushes sound,
Strengthens even the weakest,
Empowers,
Withstands all.

Gives warmth to the faithful,
Not the disloyal,
Archway never fades, never falls
Wind stops still
Over its towering steeple,
All worries are lost, forever.

Rosie Lowther (9)
Westbourne Primary School

Tree

Like a strong athlete,
As tall as a Harlem Globetrotter,
A waving, bending ballerina,
Tree, giver of health.

Shaun-Peter Wells (9)
Westbourne Primary School

Lonely Churchyard

Standing still though misty air,
Dark and dusty,
Wind whistles gently in my ears,
Gravestones bent.
Musty ivy round them like raging spirits,
Willow trees grand, steeple tall like a forgotten world,
It stands so tall and calm.
Flint walls like stones out from a raging waterfall,
A place of remembrance
In the middle of the village,
Gleaming candles all around.
The bell tower rings. Bravery surrounds me.
Bluebells scattered all around,
Writing engraved in gold.
Shadows stand tall as I sit down.

Katie Bowers (8)
Westbourne Primary School

Tree

Looks like a huge, gnarled ogre,
As it whispers messages of good times
And hums tunes of hard work,
Its leaves symbolise clean air.
Green tree, a breath of life.

Lara Stevenson (10)
Westbourne Primary School

Green Friend

He is a green friend of mine,
A kind and gentle person.
I know that he has his problems,
I know he's from a shooting star.
He is so careful with things,
He would not hurt a fly.
I know his feelings,
I know what he does,
He feels just like me when I am sad,
He just wants a friend
And he has found me.
I know his future,
I know because he tells me.
He is a green friend of mine,
A kind and gentle person.

Marc Noble (8)
Westbourne Primary School

Forest

Like a city in America,
A huge, great *tower*.
A city, but not a city.
Trees are like a resort hotel . . .
For animals.

Justin Clark (11)
Westbourne Primary School

The Holy Place

The dusty steeple stands tall for millions of years,
With a spinning cockerel on the very top, touching the sky.
The yew trees whistle in my ears,
Silent as snow melting,
The yews never fall.
The never-dying archway never fades,
We pray and worship in the very holy place.

Paige Markham (9)
Westbourne Primary School

Hands

Hands can say hello,
Can help and comfort others.
Hands can wave goodbye.

Hands can stay quite still,
But have fingers that wiggle.
We choose which they do.

Hands can hold a lot,
Hands can grip and write.

Hands can push and pull,
They can show how much you care,
But they can hurt, too.

Oliver Pescott (9)
Westbourne Primary School

HAND HAIKUS

Hands are beautiful,
Like a butterfly up high,
Ball safe in his hands.

Hands can hold wonder,
Hands can punch and be cruel,
Hands save your lifetime.

My hands can be kind,
Hands can wriggle and tie knots,
Hands can say goodbye.

Jack Reed (9)
Westbourne Primary School

PRAISE IS

Praise is bringing, singing, pleasing
In a bad world.
From a high, windy tower,
Brolly beneath a shower,
Anyone can praise.
Let us all raise,
Let us give praise
For the beauty of our Earth.

Robert Zerbini (9)
Westbourne Primary School